THE ART OF
JOYFUL LIVING

J.S. Mishra, an engineering graduate from IIT Roorkee and a former Indian Administrative Service officer, has been widely acclaimed as a competent administrator, an enabling leader, an effective writer and a passionate poet.

He has authored over two dozen books, including seven collections of Hindi poems, an anthology of English poems, a book on happiness titled *Happiness Is a Choice: Choose to Be Happy*, one on Gita, *Art of Life: Timeless Wisdom from the Gita* and five others. He has received numerous literary awards, state honours and citations for his scholarly and meritorious achievements in professional as well as literary fields.

At the moment, he serves as Chancellor, Sushant University, Gurugram, Haryana.

THE ART OF JOYFUL LIVING

J.S. Mishra

Published by
Rupa Publications India Pvt. Ltd 2023
7/16, Ansari Road, Daryaganj
New Delhi 110002

Sales centres:
Bengaluru Chennai Hyderabad
Jaipur Kathmandu Kolkata
Mumbai Prayagraj

Copyright © J. S. Mishra 2023

The views and opinions expressed in this book are the
author's own and the facts are as reported by him which have been verified to
the extent possible, and the publishers are not in
any way liable for the same.

All rights reserved.
No part of this publication may be reproduced, transmitted,
or stored in a retrieval system, in any form or by any means,
electronic, mechanical, photocopying, recording or otherwise,
without the prior permission of the publisher.

P-ISBN: 978-93-5702-580-5
E-ISBN: 978-93-5702-581-2

First impression 2023

10 9 8 7 6 5 4 3 2 1

The moral right of the author has been asserted.

Printed in India

This book is sold subject to the condition that it shall not, by way
of trade or otherwise, be lent, resold, hired out, or otherwise circulated,
without the publisher's prior consent, in any form of binding
or cover other than that in which it is published.

Contents

Preface vii

PART 1: HAPPINESS IS A CHOICE
1 Happiness Is a Choice 3
2 Zest and Affection 8
3 The Middle Path 13
4 Do What You Love 17
5 We Can Change Our Life 21
6 Celebrate Life 27
7 Meaningful Interaction 32
8 Family Is Everything 38
9 Choice of Friends 45
10 Creativity Elevates 51

PART 2: HAPPINESS IS POSSIBLE
11 If You Think, You Can 59
12 To Love and Be loved 65
13 The Need of a Soulmate 70
14 The Greatest Wealth 76
15 Enjoy Every Moment 82
16 Duty of Being Happy 90
17 The Purpose of Life 94
18 Be Your Best 99

19	A Matter of Choice	107
20	Life Is Bliss	112

PART 3: CHOOSE HAPPINESS

21	Treat Ups and Downs Alike	121
22	Pleasure Is Desirable	125
23	Memory Stored in the Heart	129
24	Today Is the Best Day	132
25	Being With Nature	135
26	Create Your Destiny	138
27	Eating Is an Art	141
28	Speaking Well Is an Art	144
29	Choose to Be Content	149
30	Joyful Existence for All	152

PART 4: THE CONQUEST OF HAPPINESS

31	Solitude Enriches Life	159
32	Listen to the Inner Voice	163
33	The Gita Can Transform Life	166
34	Pay No Attention	170
35	The Right Moment	173
36	A Spiritual Life	177
37	Meditation Transforms	180
38	Excessive Indulgence	184
39	Be Happy	189
40	Lifetime Happiness	193

Preface

Scholars all over the world are studying the art and science of happiness to enable people to lead a life of love, freedom and fulfilment. Positive psychology is nothing but a science devoted to the study of emotions and their role in enhancing happiness. The concept of positive psychology came into being around the mid-nineteenth century when scholars began studying the factors responsible for happiness.

The pursuit of happiness is every person's aspiration; in fact, the American Constitution acknowledges the pursuit of happiness as an inalienable right of every citizen. In Indian society, the main objectives of human life have been divided into four categories: *dharma*, *artha*, *kaam* and *moksha*. All of these are aimed at attaining happiness, joy and a sense of fulfilment here and hereafter. Although we use the words happiness, joy and fulfilment almost in the same breath, these are different emotions based on the degree of depth, substance and occasion.

Our happiness largely depends upon our attitude, philosophy of life and understanding of the ways of the world. In mathematical terms, happiness is equal to enjoyment (born of pleasure, a feeling derived by the senses) plus contentment plus meaning in life;

Happiness = Enjoyment + Contentment + Meaning in Life.

To be happy on a regular basis, and to enjoy life to its full potential, our endeavour should be to balance pleasure and meaning. The Nobel laureate Albert Schweitzer wrote, 'Success is not the key to happiness. Happiness is the key to success. If you love what you are doing, you will be successful.' According to a study, happy people are found to be comparatively more successful in every walk of life, including profession, health, relationship and even marriage.[*]

Charles Dickens in his famous book *A Christmas Carol and Other Christmas Writings* rightly says, 'Reflect upon your present blessings—of which every man has many—not on your past misfortunes of which all men have some.'

Therefore, another important factor in happiness is to count your blessings and not worries and misfortunes. An important contribution of positive psychology is the claim that everyone can become happy by conscious effort. It means that instead of being affected and led by feelings and emotions, we can manage and direct them towards our desired goal of a joyful life. It may be compared to working in a gym to tone our body and enhance core strength. Similarly, we can work on our feelings and emotions using the right skills, knowledge and techniques.

In the present context of society and evolution of technology, the life of an individual has become quite mechanical and fast-paced. The constant rush from home to office and back home, which becomes exhausting and monotonous, utterly drains a person of energy. He has hardly

---

[*]Lyubomirsky, S., L. King, and E. Diener, 'The Benefits of Frequent Positive Affect: Does Happiness Lead to Success?', *Psychological Bulletin*, Vol. 131, No. 6, 2005, pp. 803–855.

any occasion to feel joy and enthusiasm in this mundane routine.

The most important point in the matrix of happiness is the question whether we can change this type of dull and mundane lifestyle. This was the topmost concern in my mind when writing this book. Having discussed the issue with people of different backgrounds, ages, life experience and economic status, as well as having studied ancient scriptures and books on positive psychology, I strongly feel that the anxiety, stress and banality of life can be converted into a happy, joyful and zestful existence through conscious thoughts and determined efforts.

Another obstacle in the path of happiness is the all-pervading negative, hopeless and cynical environment that we come across in almost every interaction—in newspaper articles, on news channels and in the flood of messages we receive on social media platforms. The biggest challenge in this context is how to keep ourselves sane, unaffected and emotionally strong and fill our lives with happiness and enthusiasm.

As discussed in detail in this book, with the right intent and conscious efforts, we can overcome negativity and make our life joyful. But this would require re-evaluation of our thoughts, reorientation of our lifestyles, and resetting of the aims and objectives of our lives. Happiness will have to become a conscious priority.

We need to strengthen our mental and emotional states to walk consistently on the path of hope, joy and zest. There are various skills and methods that can be used for enhancing happiness, but one that has drawn the attention of scholars in previous decades is the model of happiness and well-being that was developed by Professor Martin Seligman, considered to be the father of positive psychology.

This model is known by its acronym, PERMA. According to this model, a joyful life can be built upon five pillars known as P-E-R-M-A, where **P** stands for positive emotions, **E** for engagement, **R** for relationship, **M** for meaning and **A** for accomplishment. Some scholars have added the letter H for health to it, as health is the most important element for joyful living and well-being.

Considering this model, we can choose a pillar or a combination of pillars depending upon the assessment of our personal specific situation, nature and habits. Almost all of us practise these pillars in our life, but to use them as a tool for happiness, we need to take a conscious decision to focus on them.

Another important factor that leads to happiness in life is the habit of sharing. A Swedish proverb says, 'Shared joy is a double joy; shared sorrow is half a sorrow.' Sharing our happiness and helping others to be happy is one of the surest ways to enjoy a life of happiness and well-being. The quote 'A rising tide lifts all boats' beautifully explains the benefits of sharing. This proverb also emphasizes that sharing problems and worries lessens their impact.

It is true that when we act in ways that make others happy, we feel happier, content and zestful. The Dalai Lama says, 'If you would like to be selfish, you should do it in a very intelligent way. The stupid way to be selfish is seeking happiness for ourselves alone. The intelligent way to be selfish is to work for the welfare of others.'

When we take care of people not related to us, a new and special type of relation evolves and in the long run yields so much joy and well-being that the initial intent of selfishness, even if it was there, totally disappears. It initiates a new relationship with a chain reaction that benefits all concerned.

Ultimately, the responsibility of being happy lies with the individual who has the option and freedom to design his life in the light of his ambitions and philosophy. Bill Burnett and Dave Evans, who teach skills and best practices for a good life, write in their book *Designing Your Life*, 'A well designed life is a life that makes sense. It is a life in which who you are, what you believe, and what you do all line up together.'

Broadly, taking good care of one's health, being surrounded by affectionate family and friends, having an assured means of livelihood, an intent to help those in distress, faith in power beyond us and viewing life events in their right perspectives are some of the ways that can make us happy and joyful. We know what make us happy; we only need to pause, reflect and work for it.

The main purpose of writing *The Art of Joyful Living* has been to urge readers to pause, think and appreciate the worth of life, the small acts of kindness and all the gifts of life that we otherwise take for granted. A new consciousness to be happy, a fresh resolve to manage life with a renewed perspective, and an attitude where each dawn is taken as a new life and each day a new beginning—these are some of the key takeaways for the readers. We must realize that it is within the reach of each of us, despite our circumstances, to not only be happy ourselves but to also make others happy and joyful.

Sincere efforts have been made to keep the chapters

small and include Learning Points at the end of each chapter to help readers grasp the essence of the content. May this book bring much joy to the readers and be a guide in their pursuit of happiness.

PART 1

HAPPINESS IS A CHOICE

Chapter 1

Happiness Is a Choice

'There is no duty we so much underrate as the duty of being happy.'
—R. L. Stevenson, Scottish writer

A healthy and happy life is within the reach of every human being. But, if we ask ten people whether they are happy, almost nine will give one reason or another for being unhappy. Very few people will accept that they are happy in life. Out of all the pursuits we strive for in life, happiness is the objective behind most of them. The American Constitution describes the pursuit of happiness as a fundamental right. Everybody wants to enjoy life and be happy, but many of us go on magnifying the problems and setbacks in our life, and hardly think about the positive aspects. This is mainly because we fail to properly understand the little and large ideas around happiness that can make us truly happy.

Taking Nothing for Granted

The cardinal principle of happiness is to understand that nothing in life should be taken for granted. We must learn the art of living with the resources at our disposal and the circumstances we are in. If we develop a healthy attitude towards ourselves and shed the burden of ego, we will find that our life is enveloped by happiness. We may find happiness while walking on a lush green lawn, gazing at the sky, or witnessing the glory of the rising sun or the grace of dusk. Rainbows, the sound of thundering clouds, the flicker of lightning and the music of raindrops—all remind us of the wonders of existence and the beauty of human life. What is needed is an attitude to relate and integrate our life with these wonders.

Happiness Is 'Just Round the Corner'

Nature is full of joy and wonder if we have the willingness and the time to pause and experience it. Simply waking up before sunrise, enjoying the chirping of birds, the freshness of the morning breeze and the feel of icy winds in the winter can fill our life with immense happiness. In fact, we are surrounded by objects of happiness, beauty and splendour, but the choice to be happy lies entirely with us. James Oppenheim, the American poet and novelist, has very rightly said, 'The foolish man seeks happiness in the distance; the wise grows it under his feet.'

The truth is that happiness is 'just around the corner' but we need to spot it, choose it, feel it and share it.

Our Attitude Matters

The surest way of being happy is to make others happy. The secret of happiness is to be large-hearted, have empathy and lead a simple life. It is a common observation that if we carry happiness within ourselves, the whole world looks beautiful and full of joy. Aldous Huxley, the English writer and philosopher, said, 'Happiness is not achieved by the conscious pursuit of happiness; it is the by-product of other activities.'

For a happy and fulfilling life, we should view life's happenings in perspective. A proper perspective changes our thought process and enables us to understand people and situations better. We should think about whether it is wiser to be happy with life or go on comparing with others and magnifying our worries, thus depriving ourselves of the joy which otherwise life has to offer.

Difficulties Are Stepping Stones

Life is a journey that is full of ups and downs. Once we realize that life will have its joys and sorrows and successes and failures, we are ready to face the difficulties and tackle the problems that we come across. If we understand that the journey of life is long and arduous, the trifles of travelling would not bother us anymore, and we will take them in our stride. A life without any hurdles or problems is bound to be quite mundane and uninteresting. It is in the game of confronting and solving the problems that life has its beauty, its worth and its meaning. These are the stepping stones that provide us with opportunities in the form of challenges and help us grow.

Accept the Problems

Human beings generally tend to ignore the problems they encounter and underestimate their magnitude. Instead of tackling problems head on, we try to skirt them and try to stay in our state of ignorant bliss. These are the reasons which cause unhappiness and make life full of tensions, anxieties and worries in the long term. Therefore, the key to happiness is to accept the problems with the right perspective, sort them out and move on.

Small Acts of Kindness

Mother Teresa has said that there are no great acts. There are only small acts done with great love. Understanding that small acts of love and kindness add happiness to the life of people around us can go a long way in creating an environment of joy and happiness. These gestures and acts make a person likeable, and, as a result, their general disposition is pleasant. Leo Tolstoy, the Russian writer, said, 'The means to gain happiness is to throw out for oneself like a spider in all directions an adhesive web of love, and to catch in all that comes.'

This is one of the greatest secrets to happiness and making other people happy.

Count Your Blessings

We do not give adequate importance to people and things in our lives, but are always acutely conscious of our deprivations and worries. We never count the gifts that life has bestowed upon us. Parental love, the co-operation and faith of our spouses, the divine gift of children, the care and concern of a true friend and the beauty and grandeur of the cosmos are the greatest gifts for a human being. Our children are the greatest gift of destiny. Giving them love and affection, and recognizing that they are the real source of happiness are some of the surest ways to make ourselves happy.

In addition to the above, a habit of cultivating friendships, enhancing one's circle of friends and well-wishers, listening to music, being one with nature, developing time discipline, reading good literature and, above all, living each day to the fullest as if it were the last, are some of the factors that can make our lives happy, joyful and meaningful.

Learning Points:

- A healthy and happy life is within the reach of every human being.
- There is no duty we so much underrate as our duty to be happy.
- Nothing in life should be taken for granted.
- Happiness is just around the corner, but we need to spot it and choose it.
- The secret of happiness is to be large-hearted and have empathy.

Chapter 2

Zest and Affection

'True happiness comes from the joy of deeds well done, the zest of creating things new.'

—Antoine de Saint-Exupery, French writer,
poet and aviator

Happiness has always been a highly valued state of existence and the pursuit of happiness has been one of the most sought-after objectives in every culture and civilization. What really makes a person happy, along with 'why' and 'how', has attracted the attention of sages, saints, scholars and commoners through the ages. The verses of sages, Vedic hymns, the wisdom of the Upanishads and modern literature on self-improvement have all shown varied paths that lead to happiness.

Happiness Is of Two Types

According to Bertrand Russell, the great philosopher and author, happiness is of two types: happiness of the heart and happiness of the head. Happiness of the heart relates to pleasure and the satisfaction of physical comfort, good health and right attitude to life. Happiness of the head pertains to the finer aspects of life, such as harmony with nature and society, and other issues of wider interest beyond one's own self and family. It also includes the ease to flow with the currents of time and the ability to accommodate the changes in life.

Zest Is Important

Zest means having great enthusiasm and energy in living one's life and attending to its different chores and activities with an extra drive. Zest is a feeling of pleasure and enthusiasm in everything that life offers. It's a quality that enables a person to derive joy and inspiration from various activities and situations happening around. It does not mean an intense or excited response to mundane aspects of life. It means having a positive and affirmative attitude towards life and towards the world. One of the most important ingredients of happiness is the zest for life, for the activities of other human being, and having zest in whatever one does or touches in one's day-to-day life.

Seeing the Good and the Beautiful

Various thinkers and philosophers have extolled the virtues of having a zestful attitude towards life. Zest is seeing the light not only at the end of tunnel but also in the initial steps when there is absolute darkness all around. It lies in finding a bright view of life and its situations and in seeing the good and the beautiful in every aspect of life and every activity. Of course, it does not mean that one is oblivious to reality. Its true essence is to have a positive and enthusiastic outlook on life, and a keen willingness to participate in life with abundant energy, passion and enthusiasm.

The World Appears Bright and Colourful

Our zest depends upon our perception of ourselves as able, competent, loved and admired person. It's a function of our belief in our skill and capabilities. If we feel we are in a position to help others or look after ourselves, it will improve our outlook towards life and instil in us confidence to take on our daily chores with enthusiasm. It leads to an awakened sense of self-confidence, security and a will to face challenges. Approval, affection and support from one's family, friends and immediate circle act as catalysts and contribute zest to one's life by validating our actions and the work that we put into our relationships. Zest makes one feel complete and accomplished. It leads to and is also increased by frequent sharing of love and affection, and it enriches one's life with health, happiness and meaning. Zest, much like happiness, depends on a feedback loop. You will receive as much as you invest. Zest makes one see the whole world as bright and beautiful.

Affection Is Life-Giving

It is common knowledge that to be happy, we need to be open and enthusiastic to life and the people we come across. We should be open and loving towards people; only then will they respond in kind. Affection and kindness have always been a two-way street. Bertrand Russel, in his famous book

The Conquest of Happiness writes that affection is reciprocally life-giving, where each side receives affection with joy, and offers it without any conscious effort, and both find the whole world much more interesting, liveable and loveable. In contrast, when one side receives affection without reciprocating, the resulting environment is not conducive to happiness, and as a result, both the subject of affection and the sender end up suffering and feeling miserable instead of being happy.

Obstacles to Happiness

The greatest obstacle in the flow of affection is ego, which hinders and obstructs the realization of happiness. Our ego prevents us from thinking about others, which is paramount when it comes to being affectionate and mindful towards others. Ego makes us retreat into ourselves, and not pay attention to anything outside of us, like other people, nature and the beauty of the world, things that are essential to being happy. In addition to ego, other major obstacles to reciprocal affection are social customs, taboos and childhood experiences. The ethical and moral value systems of society, by virtue of their repressive nature, create impediments in the path of a happy and enthusiastic attitude towards life.

Learning Points:

- The pursuit of happiness is one of the most sought-after objectives.
- Zest is one of the most important ingredients of happiness.
- Zest is seeing the good and the beautiful in every aspect of life.
- Affection is reciprocally lifegiving, where it is received with joy and offered without any conscious effort.
- The greatest obstacle in the flow of affection is the existence of ego.

Chapter 3

The Middle Path

'The Middle Path is the practice of avoiding both extremes and finding the balance that leads to wisdom.'

—The Buddha, ascetic and religious teacher

It is age-old wisdom that one should avoid extremes. It is said that excess of everything is bad, and that one should adopt a path of moderation and lead a life of awakened consciousness. Lord Buddha in his precept of *Madhyam Marg* (Middle Path) propounded the concept of moderation in life.

There is an interesting story regarding the Middle Path. Having learnt of meditation and the achievement of nirvana through severe austerity and suffering, the Buddha had almost reduced himself to a skeleton while meditating, refusing all food and rest. One day, a woman named Sujata came to him and offered a bowl of '*kheer*', a milk–rice pudding. She beseeched him to consume it, but Gautama ignored her and continued meditating. Bemused by his refusal, Sujata started singing a song about how one must tune a veena just right, not too tight nor too loose, to get the best music. The song was revelatory to Gautama. The essence of the song was that one should not tighten the strings of life's veena so much that the strings get broken, and not keep it so loose so that no music emanates from it. It is said that this incident influenced the Buddha to propound the concept of the Middle Path.

Living Like a Lotus

The Middle Path of the Buddha does not suggest only moderation but has a far greater and deeper meaning. It denotes an awakened state of mind where one is not affected by the trials and tribulations of human life, while at the same time, one is not so removed as to be unbothered about humanity and the people around us. It's akin to living like a lotus in that it is in constant touch with water but never gets wet. It's a way of life where one lives in the world but neither gets too removed from it nor is trapped in its desires and temptations.

The concept of balance and moderation had earlier been emphasized in the Bhagavad Gita. It propounds the concept of *sthit-prajna*, a state of moderate and balanced disposition. The word 'sthit-prajna' in Sanskrit means 'content and calm but firm in wisdom and discretion'. One who is not overwhelmed by the ups and downs of life and is content within himself is known as sthit-prajna. Such a person is free from worldly concerns and is fully immersed in his self.

A Balanced Life

Happiness requires balanced decision-making and deft handling of life's situations without being deterred by adversities. Both concepts indicate a way of life where one is not unduly affected by joy and sorrow, profit and loss or heat and cold. One is above these emotions and distractions. Such a person can travel the passage of life in a calm and steady manner and enjoy genuine happiness.

Equanimity Is Not Easy

The Bhagavad Gita tells the importance of transcending the dualities of life and treating success and failure as well as joy and sorrow alike. It introduces the concept of yoga and says that yoga is nothing but the art of treating the ups and downs of life in a calm and detached manner. The skill is to develop an attitude of equanimity and treat joy and suffering alike without being affected by them.

But to practise equanimity and rise above the dualities of life is not an easy task. The conduct of a person is said to be an expression of his thought process and innate nature. If one is calm and quiet, one's outward countenance will be pleasant, steady and peaceful. But the behaviour of a person having an agitated mind will be erratic and unsteady. As is the case with other things related to happiness, equanimity begins with an inward change.

Life of the Middle Path

To be happy one must have a realistic view of life and the world. The Middle Path of the Buddha advocates avoiding extremes, and exhorts the virtues of balance in life. It denotes a life where extremes of self-indulgence and self-denial are avoided. It amounts to living a moderate life where both overindulgence in pleasures and worldly affairs as well as severe asceticism are equally shunned and avoided.

Learning Points:

- One should avoid extremes.
- Middle Path is a way of life where one lives in the world but one is neither removed from it nor is trapped in desires and temptations.
- For a happy life, extremes of self-indulgence and self-denial both should be avoided.
- One should live like a lotus in the water that is in constant touch with water but neither gets wet nor is affected by it.

Chapter 4

Do What You Love

'Choose a job you love, and you will never have to work a day in your life.'
—Confucius, Chinese philosopher

The attitude of a person towards work is a crucial factor for his happiness. Whether work should be considered a cause of happiness is not an issue of debate today, since a vast majority of us, whether at home or at an office, are engaged in some work or the other for a substantial part of our day. Being busy and engaged in work one likes keeps boredom away and prevents feelings of depression and emptiness. Work provides opportunities and resources for worldly acclaim and material benefits. In addition, creative and interesting activities that are intellectually satisfying lead to genuine happiness. Such activities are the cause of happiness not only for those who are performing or producing it but also for the people who consume it.

Work as a Source of Happiness

Activities that are artistic in nature and intellectually challenging are tremendously invigorating. Works of art, literature, music, science and other fine arts can be listed in this category of activities as they increase one's zest for life by bringing in change, engagement and colour. Such activities demand time, energy and resources from the person who undertakes it but provide a great sense of accomplishment. In fact, these engagements do not remain mere activities; rather, they become the ultimate source of happiness. Writing a poem, painting a portrait or landscape, composing some music or some profound discovery by a scientist cannot be confined within the definition of work, but rather, such activities eventually become a great source of happiness and inspiration to all.

Work as an Act of Prayer

The essence of happiness is to find out what type of activity really excites a person. What one genuinely loves to do. Once such activities are identified, for happiness, one should devote full energy in accomplishing it.

Work may not always bring joy to us, but without work there will never be any joy or happiness in life. Happiness is not always performing great tasks or creating widely acclaimed pieces of art; rather, it can be found even in routine chores when they are approached with love and devotion, as an act of prayer. If we concentrate on the long term, even the most mundane tasks can give us an enormous sense of self-fulfilment and achievement at the end of the day and week. It will also help us tide over the monotony of work and related boredom.

In the poem 'On Work' from his famous book *The Prophet*, Kahlil Gibran underlines the importance of work:

> You work that you may keep pace with the earth
> and the soul of the earth.
> For to be idle is to become a stranger unto the
> seasons,
> and to step out of life's procession,
> that marches in majesty and proud submission
> towards the infinite.

Work Is Love Made Visible

Prima facie, the fact that work and love are related appears to be an act of poetic imagination. But if we ponder over the implications of work in all its possible dimensions, we find that the beauty, comfort and progress in civilization is the result of research, innovation and the endeavours of people who worked with focus, dedication and love.

To work with love has been aptly highlighted in the same poem as above:

> Work is love made visible.
> And if you cannot work with love but only with
> distaste, it is better that you should leave your work
> and sit at the gate of the temple and take alms of
> those who work with joy.

Probably the poet does not mean that people should stop working and start begging. The central theme of the poem is that whatever is to be done as part of one's work should be done with love, and in such a way that it becomes a source of joy and fulfilment. If it is not possible, one should try to change it and seek an assignment that ignites one's passion and brings the best out of one.

Do What You Love

It is true that one can become an accomplished performer in any area if he works with love and dedication. Any work performed with love and excitement is highly rewarding. Gloria Steinem says, 'Without leaps of imagination, or dreaming, we lose the excitement of possibilities. Dreaming after all, is a form of planning.'

There is an inner urge in every human being to excel, win and accomplish in order to gain recognition, success and be happy. The secret of happiness is to choose an activity one loves to do, and then do one's best at it. Happiness is nothing but liking what you are doing, and liking how you are doing it. The perception that you are doing something important and exciting gives real joy and happiness in life.

Learning Points:

- The attitude towards work is a very crucial factor for happiness.
- Happiness is nothing but liking what you are doing, and the way you are doing it.
- Happiness is doing even routine chores with love and dedication.
- Any work performed with love and excitement is highly rewarding.
- The secret of happiness is to choose an activity you love to do, and then doing it with a drive.

Chapter 5

We Can Change Our Life

*'Your vision will be clear when you can look into your heart.
Who looks outside, dreams; who looks inside, awakes.'*

—Carl Jung, Swiss psychoanalyst and psychiatrist

One of the most puzzling questions before humans today is how to realize and maximize one's happiness. The hunger for more money, comfort, security, prestige, name and fame, everything more than what we already have is the real barrier in the quest for happiness.

Most of us are blinded by a distorted notion of success and are running a mad race without realizing its consequences. It is a race without well-defined destinations and is causing tremendous stress and an acute sense of insecurity. This is leading to a stressful lifestyle devoid of any method or meaning, which negatively affects not just our mental health but also our physical health in the long run.

The Never-Ending Preparation

All of us try to be happy in accordance with our own view of life. Most of the things that make us sad and unhappy are quite often self-chosen. Most of the time, we are responding to our basic instincts on the spur of the moment without regarding the consequences of our choices. We devote our time and energy in the pursuit of mundane and trivial things, making efforts to acquire material objects that we believe will make us happy one day. We are not living; rather we are forever planning, acquiring, collecting and preparing to live. We are drawn into a never-ending preparation to live.

There Are Always Choices

We neither have the time nor intention to give a serious thought to the choices and decisions available to us. The things and activities that make us feel elevated, joyous and upbeat never get priority in our thought process. Whether it is a choice between putting in more hours at work, attending late-night dinners, earning more money and means of comfort, or of being with our children, sharing time with them, listening to music, reading good literature, watching the starlit sky, the question of which will be more rewarding never arises.

The choices are open to all of us, but we are neither aware of them nor conscious of them. In the present context of life, we do not contemplate over these issues. And when some of us do it, often it can be quite late.

Live the Life of Your Dreams

Our restricted vision and internal resistance to new ideas along with the fear to march on the unfrequented path are major obstacles in achieving happiness. We do not live up to our full potential and possibilities. We are afraid of new thoughts and new paths. We feel comfortable in walking on familiar tracks. To live life to its full potential, it is essential that we do not waste our time and energy in mere survival; rather we should make our best efforts to live the life of our dreams.

It is said that about 60,000 thoughts cross our minds in a day; most of them are mere repetitions as these thoughts were there yesterday, and most probably will engage our mind and attention again tomorrow. Without new thoughts and innovative actions, there cannot be any joy and enthusiasm in life. The lack of new vision and fresh thinking results in a boring, mundane and monotonous life.

New Vision and New Thoughts

New vision and new thoughts are required to make life happy and zestful. In this context, Jonas Salk, the American virologist who developed the polio vaccine, says, 'I have had dreams, and I have had nightmares. I overcame the nightmares because of my dreams.' To be open to new ideas is the key to a meaningful life. What we achieve in life largely depends on our thoughts and the decisions we make. Happiness is a result of our dreams, thoughts and our responses to them. Thought management and sensitivity to thought-triggers lead to success and happiness in life. To be happy, we need to be awake to the wonders of our mind, see new dreams and realize them with sustained endeavours.

Take a Plunge

It has been observed that quite often, negative experiences from the past dominate our mind and restrict our ability to innovate and take initiatives. It adversely affects our risk-taking abilities as instead of availing new opportunities and responding to unfolding events with an open mind, we become prisoners of the past. We get tied to past experiences, and thus, miss many golden opportunities. The cardinal principle of happiness is to discard the baggage of the past, look forward with a new vision and take a plunge with our full might. We should be ever willing to seize the day and seize the moment.

Limitations in Vision

Our limitations do not lie as much in our abilities as in our vision. It signifies that our inability to experience happiness mostly lies in our own restricted vision; it is not a result of our external circumstances, as we would normally like to believe.

Our restricted vision about our capabilities is an obstacle in our journey to the destination of joy and happiness. We all have a great reservoir of energy to accomplish any task we set our heart to, but the greatest irony of human life is that most of us are not aware of it. That is why the scriptures, poets, reformers and philosophers emphasize the need to reach the inner recesses of our mind and soul in order to expand our vision and fulfil our capabilities.

Move beyond Comfort Zones

We like to live within the confines of our comfort zone and there always is an inherent resistance to new challenges and new paths. But to have a life of joy and meaning, it is essential to move beyond our comfort zones. All human accomplishments have been the result of transcending comfort zones, indulging in new endeavours and crossing known boundaries. The ascent to Mount Everest, the advent of the steam engine, electric bulb, wireless, telephone, mobile technology, AI and millions of other inventions and discoveries were possible only because people had vision, thoughts and perseverance to transcend the known confines and look beyond what already existed.

The Master Key to Happiness

The world around us is nothing but a reflection of our wishes, fears, dreams and fantasies. It reflects what we have within us. Our reactions, responses, behaviour and inclination towards life depend on our inner state of mind. We can change the course of our life through new vision, new thoughts and new dreams. Altering our thoughts and attitudes, we can change our life, and not only lead a happy and joyful life but also affect the life of others and make them happy.

The secret of happiness lies in knowing oneself and one's potential, and then thinking of new ways, new paths and new milestones. Life is all about finding our true calling which elevates and provides joy and happiness to us, and then directing our total energy towards achieving it. To find out what's close to one's heart is the master key to happiness.

Learning Points:

- One of the most important challenges in life is how to realize and maximize happiness.
- We are forever planning, acquiring, collecting and preparing to live.
- We feel comfortable in walking on tracks frequented through ages.
- About 60,000 thoughts cross our minds in a day, most of them are mere repetitions.
- New vision and new thoughts are required to make life happy and zestful.

Chapter 6

Celebrate Life

'There are only two ways to live your life. One is as though nothing is a miracle. The other is as though everything is a miracle.'

—Albert Einstein, German theoretical physicist

Mahabharata, the great epic of Ancient India, describes the main ingredients of happiness. The factors which constitute a life full of joy and happiness, have been beautifully enumerated in the following *shloka*:

Arogya, anrinya, avipravasah,
Sadbhih manushyaih saha samprayogah,
Sva pratyaya vrittir abheet vasah,
Shad jivalokasya sukhani rajan.

[Perfect health, free from debt, living with one's kith and kin, company of virtuous people, reliable means of livelihood and absence of fear; these six constitute a life full of joy and happiness.]*

---

*All translations of Indian texts are author's own unless stated otherwise.

Something Is Missing

A perfect state of health, reliable means of livelihood, staying with family, interaction with learned people and sense of security have been traditionally seen as the factors supposed to make anybody happy and content with life. These parameters were relevant even in the early stages of civilization, when life was not as safe, secure and comfortable as it is today. In the present context of living, it is common observation that despite a good quality of life, security and recognition, something still seems to be missing in many people's lives. Most people feel a lack of contentedness and a sense of emptiness. Making life joyful, vibrant and interesting is a great challenge in the present context of life.

Happiness Is Culture-Centric

If we can take life in a balanced manner without getting upset with its ups and downs, we can be happy and joyful. To be happy, our mind should be stable and tranquil to such an extent that unpleasant and untoward incidents are not able to disturb it.

The key to a balanced state of mind depends on our own concept of good and bad, joy and sorrow, gain and loss. This ultimately depends on our attitude towards life and the philosophy of life. To a large extent, happiness is quite culture-centric and depends on our surroundings and upbringing. Some cultures profess seriousness in life and attach a lot of virtue to it, whereas certain societies take life as it comes on a day-to-day basis, and live life in the most enthusiastic way.

Celebrate Life

In a way, every day should be an occasion to be happy and celebrate life. To celebrate life means that anything we do should be done not as a duty, or as a burden, or as something drab and dull; rather, it should be done with full energy and enthusiasm. Children and young people in every society love being carefree, and indulge in laughing, dancing, singing and celebrating life on every pretext. But as one advances in age, life's burdens, customs, rituals, and the general ethos of society take over one's life and the occasions to celebrate become increasingly less.

Laughter Is the Best Medicine

It is interesting to note that of all species, only human beings can laugh and express their happiness. Laughter is a spontaneous response of a human being to express joy and happiness. Laughter is said to be an immediate mood booster. It may have a very transitory existence but has the potential to lift the mood of a gathering. Laughter is the culmination and expression of happiness which spreads joy all around.

Too Serious to Enjoy

The predisposition to be joyful is a factor of culture and environment, which in turn is largely affected by the history and geography of people. In our society, there is an inherent resistance to free and spontaneous expressions of joy. This is a great obstacle to feeling happy and exuberant.

The Moment to Celebrate

Celebration of life must not succumb to extraneous forces. One can celebrate life at any moment. To celebrate life, only the right attitude and inclination and a conscious decision to do so are needed. When we celebrate life, joy and happiness become self-perpetuating. One should not be bogged down with difficulties and postpone celebration. In fact, ideal conditions never exist in life. If we go on postponing the celebration and waiting for an ideal condition, eventually it becomes a way of life and traps us in a self-defeating cycle. The moment to celebrate never comes.

Every Man a King, Every Woman a Queen

Bertrand Russell has described in his book *The Conquest of Happiness* his experience of visiting a tribal community living deep in a forest. He was surprised to see their zest for living and celebrating life. After working hard in the day, members of the community danced the whole night, and once fully tired, fell asleep on the ground on which they were dancing. By the next morning, they were up again to go back to their work. Their routine of working the whole day and celebrating life at night went on unabated almost all days of the month. The crowns they wore were not of gold or silver, but of leaves and flowers, yet every man in the group behaved like a king and every woman a queen.

Learning Points:

- Most of the people feel lack of contentedness and a sense of emptiness in life.
- Making life joyful, vibrant and interesting is a great challenge in the present context of life.
- Happiness is a function of our attitude, mental disposition and view of life.
- Every day should be an occasion to be happy and celebrate life.
- If we go on postponing celebrations, it becomes a way of life.

Chapter 7

Meaningful Interaction

'Man is by nature a social animal; an individual who is unsocial naturally and not accidentally is either beneath our notice or more than human.'

—Aristotle, Greek philosopher

Man cannot live alone as his basic nature is to relate and seek interactions that reduce the feeling of isolation and the fear of being alone. The absence of meaningful interaction makes life dull and mundane. In such situations, mobile, television, films and cocktail circuits remain the only option of entertainment for isolated individuals. These engage attention of a person at a superficial level, and do not lead to any kind of bonding or meaningful relationships.

Basic Human Nature

Social interaction is basic to human nature. Even while travelling by public transport, people seated together cannot be silent for long. Very soon they seek some reason or another to initiate interaction. But such interactions are casual and do not lead to any bonding or relationship. At social gatherings as well, there is no free flow of interaction as many people have a compulsive tendency to display their positions and possessions. In such situations, the resulting conversations acquire overtones of arrogance and hinders closeness and bonding.

Worth of a Person

The prevalent trend in society is to evaluate a person and accord importance to them not on their qualities and individual merit but rather on their status, position and worldly achievements. It makes social interactions monotonous, boring and non-participative. The true worth of a person should be measured by their personality, pursuits, interests and activities other than their means of livelihood. This can add quality, colour and substance to social interactions.

Life Taken for Granted

Most people take material acquisition as the sole aim of life, while others consider living with adequate resources and comforts as the reward for life. Their vision is limited to having a good house, fancy car and enough wealth to live comfortably. This is all they think of life. A life limited to physical comforts and material possessions only cannot be called enriching and meaningful. Most people confuse livelihood with living. The main reason for this situation in our society is that we do not value life but rather take it for granted. We go through life almost mechanically without examining its purpose and meaning or without seriously evaluating the way we are leading our lives.

Meaningful Interaction

The fact of life remains that meaningful social interaction is of great importance for a joyful and meaningful existence. Interaction with cultured persons with whom one is able to talk comfortably is an important component for a joyful life. However, this calls for a certain type of social environment.

It was possible when there was less movement of people to new places having different customs, traditions and culture. People spent their life in a known and familiar social and cultural setting. In such situations, the people one met with, were known, familiar and provided better opportunities for social mingling and interactions. But the rapid growth of urbanization has given rise to unorganized and inorganic societies that hinder easy flow of mixing and enriching interactions.

It is a common observation that social life with urbane and polite people has now become quite rare—even extinct. The belief in the dictum of struggle for existence and survival of the fittest might have contributed to the creation of wealth, but it has quite adversely affected the charm and sweetness of social life.

Interesting Social Life Is Vital

An interesting social life is a vital element for a happy and meaningful social existence. Social life is nothing but natural flowing and mingling of people having different personality traits and possessing different educational and cultural backgrounds. This leads to a free and cultured sharing of thoughts and ideas, and results in harmony and meaningful relationships.

In social gatherings, one meets new people, socializes with them and derives cues for one's own growth and development. In addition to the above, social trends, fashion trends and cultural demeanour provide adequate exposure to a person of keen interest and observation. Therefore, the need for a proper social gathering is one of the most important and critical factors for happiness in life.

Interacting Is a Great Art

Another important factor in developing a meaningful social life is the style and substance of interactions. Interacting is a great art and enhances not only the acceptability and popularity of a person but also adds dignity and prestige to the person concerned. Therefore, for a joyful life, a free and amicable environment and enriching social interaction is very important. It adds richness and sophistication to society and is the cumulative aggregate of the individual behaviour of its members.

Be Cautious

There are occasions when social interactions become a part of custom and social obligation. We must be careful on such occasions as social relations at best should be a source of mutual convenience and never become a burden. However, one should try to participate in such gatherings as habitual absence attracts ridicule and criticism in society. Participation on such occasions enhances social acceptability and results in closeness and belonging. If one can conduct oneself properly, it may even lead to appreciation.

Be Selective in Interactions

An important aspect of happiness in social life is to be highly selective in one's social interactions. Well-thought-out and selective social interaction with agreeable people is often much more rewarding. Ultimately, one must find happiness from within and should not depend on others for one's happiness. If a person does not have their own reasons to be happy, no social interaction can make up for it and act as a substitute.

The sum and substance of social interaction and cultivation of relationships is that one should interact with persons one feels comfortable and enthusiastic with, and with whom one shares tastes and hobbies.

Learning Points:

- Man cannot live alone, as his basic nature is to relate and seek interactions.
- Interaction reduces the feeling of isolation and the fear of being alone.
- The prevalent trend in society is to evaluate a person not on their qualities and merit but rather on their status, position and worldly achievements.

- A life limited to physical comforts and material possessions cannot be called enriching and meaningful.
- The true worth of a person should be measured by their personality, pursuits and interests rather than their means of livelihood.

Chapter 8

Family Is Everything

'In family life, love is the oil that eases friction, the cement that binds closer together, and the music that brings harmony.'

—Friedrich Nietzsche, German philosopher

The concept of family has existed since the dawn of civilization. The family is regarded as the cornerstone of society, as it forms the basic unit of social organization. It is seen as a multi-functional institution and is indispensable for social life. The institution is necessary for the initiation of young members into society to learn familial responsibilities, customs and social traditions. The family has become an inevitable component of human life.

The essential features of family are that members live together, pool their resources and work together for common goals. The structure of a family varies from society to society. The smallest family unit is the unitary or nuclear family, which consists of the head of the family, spouse and their children. Larger family units are known as joint families and are extensions of the basic nuclear unit.

Evolved over Centuries

Nuclear families are solely dependent upon their own resources and many times behave like an overloaded electrical circuit. The demands piling up on an individual from family, society and environment are tremendous and hard to cope with. The chances of fuses blowing are high as the family members expect and demand too much from one another. This situation prima facie does not appear to be conducive for a happy and balanced life. But the family system has evolved over centuries and has worked well. Despite tremendous stress and strain, it provides adequate space and ample opportunities for everybody's growth and happiness in the family.

Passing through a Critical Phase

Family is the root cause and most important focus of human endeavour in society. But the institution of family now is passing through a critical phase. Today, the family system is increasingly becoming a source of irritation and unhappiness. Earlier, family life meant the existence of a joint family system, but now it largely means a unitary family. In our society, children are an integral part of the family till they complete their education, get employed and settle down with their own families.

Family: An Exalted Institution

The family has traditionally been an exalted institution. It is considered the basic unit in achieving the four main objectives of life, namely *dharma*, *arth*, *kaam* and *moksha*. It means that all worldly achievements as well as spiritual attainments were thought to be possible within the family system. Earlier, the joint family was a general norm but now it has become an exception. The concept of a joint family was helpful for a balanced and enriching life. A joint family provided an environment in which children learnt etiquette or how to behave with others and how to be accommodating or large-hearted as they lived with several generations in one home.

Unitary Family Now Prominent

The joint family system can be a great lesson in sharing, accommodating and adjusting to other individuals in the family. During festivals, wedding ceremonies and other occasions people had more fun as compared to a family of three or four members. The joint family system was also a great social security mechanism, because if a tragedy occurred, other family members stepped up to take care of the safety, security and other basic needs of the surviving members.

Therefore, the joint family system provided an opportunity for two or three generations to thrive together. The system had many advantages, but it hindered individual growth and witnessed conflicts due to jealousy and bickering among family members. That is why the unitary family system gained prominence.

The Young Prefer Unitary System

The joint family system is not totally out of favour. In fact, due to economic pressure and the desire to lead a quality life, in families where both spouses are working, the revival of the joint family system is finding favour. It takes care of the safety and security aspect as well as provides a healthy family environment for the children and aged alike.

It is difficult to conclude whether a unitary or joint family system is more amenable to ensure happiness in the family. Happiness does not depend on the type of family system per se; it depends on the upbringing, economic and social status and the aims and objectives of the family. Today, the young generation considers the unitary family system to be better as it gives freedom and space to members for self-growth and advancement.

Positive Environment Needed

The role of family as an institution in enhancing the happiness and well-being of its members has been universally accepted. There is absolutely no doubt that for a happy existence, the institution of family is quite helpful. But its success depends upon the environment and co-operation of all family members. To fulfil the objectives of a family as ordained in the ancient scriptures, there should be a positive environment to promote co-operation and understanding among family members.

Vitality Is Important

Vitality is very important for the happiness of the family. Even a single member lacking vitality may adversely affect the environment of a family. But it is also true that even one highly charged and super active family member can electrify the family environment and lead to peace, prosperity and happiness. This person can act as a leading light of the group and prove to be the captain of the ship. If other family members can generate enthusiasm and play their roles responsibly, such a family is not only able to face the storm and cover distances but is also able to discover new avenues for itself.

The Issue of Space

Another important attribute of a happy and successful family is the environment of enthusiasm and dynamism in the family. The issue of space is also very important for its success. There should be adequate space for living a happy and healthy life for every member. Exuberant and high-spirited members as well as those more sober should be able to live together and enjoy equal importance. Members need to accommodate and appreciate the role of others in order to co-exist happily. The sense of accommodation and co-existence is the essence of happiness and success for a family.

Familial Co-Operation

It is obvious that willing co-operation of every member is essential for a happy and successful family. It can generate a magnetic field of love, affection and respect in the family, and for such a family no goal is too high and no destination is too far. But the cardinal principle remains that every member of the family must contribute their best, keeping in view the overall interest of the family.

Need for Discipline

For a happy and balanced family, there is a need for discipline and order to ensure that everybody contributes according to their ability, and derives benefits as per their needs. Each member must co-operate with the head of the family. Otherwise, there is indiscipline and chaos in the family, leading to distress, conflict and unhappiness.

Children Have Their Own Thoughts

An often-observed phenomenon is the will of parents to make their children behave according to what they perceive is the right behaviour. There is a general tendency among parents to make the child a living replica of themselves. This not only causes tremendous stress on the psyche of a child but also sows the seeds of conflict in the family.

It is important that children get guidance and assistance from their parents but they should be free to make their own decisions and shape their life.

Kahlil Gibran in the poem 'On Children' in his famous book *The Prophet* describes the importance of freedom for children in the family:

Your children are not your children.
They are the sons and daughters of life's longing for itself.
They come through you but not from you,
And though they are with you yet they belong not to you.
You may give them your love but not your thoughts,
For they have their own thoughts.

Learning Points:

- The family is seen as a multi-functional institution and is indispensable for social life.
- Despite tremendous stress and strain, a family provides adequate space and ample opportunities for growth and happiness.
- A joint family provides an environment in which children learn etiquette and the benefits of co-operation.
- In families where both spouses are working, the joint family system takes care of the safety and security aspect and provides a healthy environment for the children and aged alike.
- Children should get guidance and assistance from parents but should be free to make their own decisions.

Chapter 9

Choice of Friends

'Friendship improves happiness, and abates misery, by doubling our joys, and dividing our grief.'

—Marcus Tullius Cicero,
Roman statesman & philosopher

A friend is someone whom one knows, likes and trusts. A friend is there to share, rejoice and support. A friend should be one with whom one can comfortably confide, and whose opinions are valued for their sheer sincerity. The great Roman philosopher Cicero said that friendship improves happiness and abates misery by doubling our joys and dividing our grief. Therefore, friendship should grow gently and gradually because if it is rushed it may soon run out of breath. To have a true and genuine friend is a great asset. We should make our best effort to choose friends with whom we can share our joy and grief freely. To choose and be chosen as a friend is one of the greatest joys in life.

Test in Adversity

Life is never a bed of roses. There are twists and turns, ups and downs, and bright and dark patches all along the path of life. There may be many near and dear ones based on blood and marriage relationships, social bonding, and other societal obligations, but one needs somebody who can be a soulmate, a friend in hours of joy as well as adversities. It is true that the real test of genuine friendship is during the adversities of life.

In the epic *Ramcharitmanas*, the great poet Tulsi Das describes the virtues of a true friend in the following lines:

> *Dheeraj dharam, mitra aru naree,*
> *Aapad kaal parkhiye charee.*
>
> [One should test his patience, right conduct, friends and wife during the times of crisis.]

Friends Are Always Needed

The sense of having a true friend gives great strength and creates a reservoir of energy and enthusiasm. It contributes immensely to good health and happiness. Apart from family members, friends provide the greatest joy and motivation. Presence of a close friend promotes health and is a great buffer against sorrow and depression. Life being what it is, friends are needed in times of both joy and sorrow.

It has been observed that those who enjoy close relationships generally feel better, exercise more and enjoy life. In fact, a trustworthy friendship expedites recovery during acute sickness and enhances self-confidence and self-esteem. In hours of adversity, timely advice, reassurance and presence of a true friend act as a great medicine and boosts our morale.

Friends Act as a Buffer

The rise of individualism has led to an era of individual freedom and pride in one's achievements. In the course of life, we come across setbacks and failures, and the main accountability falls on the individual concerned, as one must own up to it and take responsibility and suffer the consequences alone. Living as an individual who exercises his own choices and takes decisions, there are occasions when one feels trapped and totally lost. In such situations, the presence of a sincere friend acts as a buffer in absorbing the shocks and motivates one towards a new initiative, a new life.

When Lightning Strikes

The traditional support of a family, community or other larger social groups in the eventuality of setbacks and personal tragedies is gradually declining. One is left to fend for oneself. Today, the cardinal principle of life is to live as per one's own choice and convictions. This has become the culture of the day. It leaves one lonely in the struggle of life. In such an environment, when lightning strikes, there is no shelter, no roof and no support group, which can be the cause behind depression and feelings of being demotivated. Lack of a concrete support system can also lead to low self-esteem, which pulls a person inward into themselves and reluctant to seek friends, therefore leading to a vicious circle of suffering and sadness.

To Share and Support

In the present context, individualism has become fully ingrained in the human psyche. In moments of success, one feels on top of the world and derives pride and happiness. The basic instinct is to take full credit and internalize this feeling as well. So far, so good. But in the event of hurt, disgrace and major setbacks, there being no family or support system to fall back upon, one feels stressed, depressed and helpless. In this vulnerable situation, a person needs a friend who can genuinely share their sorrows and provide support and comfort.

If one has close friends to relate and share one's personal issues with confidence, one is in a privileged position. In a survey conducted in the US, it was found that people having five or six friends with whom they could discuss important matters were 60 per cent more likely to feel 'very happy' as compared to those who had none.

To Be Chosen with Care

Friends should be chosen with full knowledge about the quality of the person, their personality, interests and leanings. One should not rush while selecting a friend. One should also not be in the habit of consulting a friend for everything in life, as people are ever willing to advise in the light of their own interests and perspectives. But the real guide resides in our own being. As the popular saying goes, 'One should make fast friends, but not friends fast.'

We carry the blueprint, the road map of happiness and harmony, in our being. The secret is to understand, identify and try to take an informed decision while choosing a friend.

Trust Is Important

To be intimate and friendly, one must understand the crucial role of trust in friendship. These days, the basic instinct to trust and be trustworthy has become quite rare. There is the all-pervading falsehood and deceit in society. But if we genuinely develop trust in a friend or even an acquaintance, it is highly improbable that they will cheat us. By trusting and becoming trustworthy, we raise the standard of human behaviour.

Kahlil Gibran in his poem 'On Friend' in the book *The Prophet* describes the qualities of a friend:

> Your friend is your needs answered. He is your field which you sow with love and reap with thanksgiving. And he is your board and your fireside.
> For you come to him with your hunger, and you seek him for peace.

The Art of Joyful Living

> **Learning Points:**
>
> - A friend is someone whom one knows, likes and trusts.
> - Friendship improves happiness and abates misery by doubling the joy and dividing the grief.
> - To have a true and genuine friend is a great asset.
> - Friendship should grow gently and gradually because if it is rushed, it may soon run itself out of breath.
> - By trusting and becoming trustworthy, we raise the standard of human behaviour.

Chapter 10

Creativity Elevates

'Happiness is not in the mere possession of money; it lies in the joy of achievement, in the thrill of creative effort.'

—Franklin D. Roosevelt,
American statesman and politician

A creative person is one who has insight and can see things in a way others are not able to see and can hear the voices nobody else has heard. To create, one must go beyond all barriers and conditioning and do something new, something entirely novel. It is to walk on an untrodden path, to dive into new depths, and to seek new horizons.

Creativity in essence is transcending known boundaries; it is not simply limited to painting a new picture but also in the use of a new canvas and imagining different possibilities.

Creativity Is Sublime

Creativity does not force but facilitates creation by acting as an enabler, an instrument. It is an activity where one loses one's identity and participates without consciously being the instrument. It is like a rainbow that appears without any conscious effort from the Sun. In essence, creativity is permitting something sublime, extraordinary and entirely new to happen on its own.

Letting Creativity Flow

Creativity in its true sense means that the forces involved have a free play without any conscious intervention. When poets write a poem, they are only a medium, a vehicle; not the creator but only an instrument. If they write consciously, it may still be a poem but often it is ordinary and mundane. But when it comes from beyond, it always contains something new and divine. This is how the Vedas, the Upanishads, the Quran and the Bible happened and were gifted to mankind.

Something Goes Amiss

It is said that when poet Samuel Taylor Coleridge died, he left thousands of incomplete poems. During his lifetime, he was reminded many times by his friends and well-wishers about incomplete poems as some of his poems needed only a line or two to be complete. But he could never complete them and the poems remained unfinished.

When asked, Coleridge's response described the real nature of creativity:

> I cannot. I have tried, but when I complete them, something goes amiss, something goes wrong. My line never falls in tune with that which has come through

me. It remains a stumbling block, it becomes a rock, it hinders the flow. So, I have to wait. Whosoever has been flowing through me, whenever he again starts flowing and completes the poem, it will be completed, not before that.

Coleridge completed only a few poems during his lifetime, but those poems are creations of divine beauty and have great insights.

The Power Beyond Reveals Itself

This is always the case with genuine creativity. In such situations, the artist disappears, the poet experiences a new process where he does not know how the words and feelings surged and the poem happened. It is true with every form and aspect of creation. The power beyond reveals itself through a poem, a painting or the form and curves of a sculpture. This is creativity. As a part of this mystical process, the artist experiences a strange feeling of ecstasy, a great sense of elation, which ultimately leads to a feeling of sheer joy and contentment.

Drop the Ego

For creativity, one must forget oneself and be egoless and receptive to every aspect of life and nature. The hues and colours of the rainbow, the scenic beauty of snow-clad mountains, the silence and majesty of the jungle and the whispers of a spring breeze convey profound messages and transport a receptive mind to a new reality, a new world.

Therefore, for creativity to take shape, there must be adequate space, new thoughts and keen willingness.

Become One with Life

If a person is full of themselves, harbouring thoughts and feelings that feed their ego, they can never create something great. Once we drop our ego, we become light and our anxiety and frustration drops. We give space to positivity and new strength starts flowing through us. By dropping our pretensions and ego, we easily relate with life and existence.

Ego is like a rock around our neck. The moment it vanishes, we feel weightless and peaceful, at peace with ourselves and the world. When an artist sheds ego and forgets himself, the real art takes shape. In such a scenario, he is there in the process, but does so innocently, unconsciously and unknowingly. He becomes an integral part in the process of creativity. Great art emerges when the artist disappears. This is where the road to happiness, to real joy, begins.

Elevated and Uplifted

As soon as we become egoless, we feel immensely elevated and uplifted. Quite often it happens that sitting on a beach and watching the rays of the setting sun and surging waves, or walking on difficult hilly terrain or climbing a mountain, we truly realize the transitory nature of life and the limitations of human existence. In such situations, there is a strong urge to connect with our inner being which otherwise remains dormant. We feel a sense of elevation, a relief from the mundane existence and the presence of some universal force running the affairs of the world.

Feeling of Sheer Joy

Creativity has multiple facets and different co-ordinates that define it. But invariably, it leads to genuine happiness, an exalted feeling of existence that is quite extraordinary and divine. It exhilarates, elevates and uplifts. I have myself experienced such feelings in my creative journey when a poem flows on its own without any intent or effort. Likewise, while watching the sunrise, starlit sky and full moon, I have felt being transported to a different world. Just watching the rainfall with intermittent flashes of lightning and hearing raindrops and thunder transports one to an entirely different level of existence if one is fully present and there is no distraction. It's a great experience, a divine feeling of sheer joy, the joy that permeates every pore of our being and helps us realize a new state of existence.

In order to be happy, to experience an exalted sense of joy, the importance of creativity cannot be overemphasized. The lives of great poets, saints, litterateurs and artists symbolize a great sense of joy, serenity and peace. Out of all the attributes and factors leading to genuine happiness, the role of creativity is of paramount importance.

Lasts for Generations

Writing a great poem, painting with abandon and composing immortal music—all lead to a state of ecstasy, a sense of elation and joy which is entirely divine and blissful. Creativity is unique in the sense that it has universal value that not only benefits the artist and the people around but also reaches far and wide. It remains a thing of joy forever, often lasting for generations.

> **Learning Points:**
>
> - Creativity is transcending the known boundaries, entering a new orbit and searching new worlds.
> - Creativity is not only painting a new picture but also using a new canvas and imagining a new possibility.
> - Creativity means that the forces involved have a free play without any conscious intervention.
> - For creativity, one must forget oneself, be egoless, keen and receptive to every aspect of life and nature.
> - Creativity leads to genuine happiness, an exalted feeling of existence, quite extraordinary and divine.

PART 2

HAPPINESS IS POSSIBLE

Chapter 11

If You Think, You Can

'Human beings, by changing the inner attitudes of their minds, can change the outer aspects of their lives.'

—William James, American philosopher

According to David G. Myers, author of *The Pursuit of Happiness*, self-esteem, sense of control, optimism and extraversion are four elements that predispose the positive attitude of a person. Each of these elements promotes happiness and leads to a sense of well-being. Out of this, self-esteem is the most decisive factor to affect the attitude of a person.

Self-Esteem

When life becomes tough, people with strong self-esteem keep going and very soon change their life for the better. There is a direct connection between poor self-esteem and depression. Feelings of unhappiness, frustration and depression lead to psychosomatic and neurotic symptoms. Likewise, there is a strong connection between high self-esteem and a sense of happiness and well-being. The best predictor of happiness in life is not wealth or income, friends, or family but self-esteem and the perception of one's own self-worth.

Learn to Love Yourself

It is a common experience that people who like and accept themselves as they are feel extremely good about life. That is why all the literature on self-help emphasizes the importance of respecting oneself and being conscious of one's positive points. Friedrich Wilhelm Nietzsche, the German philosopher, has said that to find love one must learn to love oneself. Positive self-esteem is a great protection against anxiety and depression, and it leads to great physical and mental health. But it should be based on realism. If it is based on proper assessment, it leads to enduring joy and sustainable happiness.

Sense of Control

The second most important attribute of a happy person is a sense of control over the affairs of their life. Angus Campbell of the University of Michigan, after extensive survey, concluded, 'Having a strong sense of control over the affairs of one's life is a more dependable predictor of positive feelings of well-being than any of the objective conditions of the life.'

He concluded that 15 per cent of the surveyed people who felt they were in full control of their lives were found to have 'extraordinary positive feelings of happiness'. If the perception of control is enhanced, there is significant improvement in the health and happiness of the person concerned.

People Thrive in Democracy

Judith Rodin, president, The Rockefeller Foundation, in her talk titled 'Public Health 2.0: Aligning People and Planet' at Yale University, says that encouraging nursing home patients to exercise their choice in the upkeep of their environment and have a say in policy framework resulted in 93 per cent of the patients becoming more alert, active and happy. It is a common belief that people thrive best under conditions of democracy where an environment of freedom and security prevails. They have a better perception of their quality of life and happiness as compared to the people living under authoritarian regimes.

Time Management

Another important element for positive attitude is the sense of effective time management. Those who are not able to plan and fill their time with worthwhile creative activities are found to be unhappy and unstable by temperament. The habit of being late in the night, excessive screen watching and having an irregular routine creates a feeling of emptiness and worthlessness. According to Michael Argyle of Oxford University, 'For happy people, time is filled and planned; they are punctual and efficient. Whereas for unhappy people, time is unfilled, open and uncommitted; they postpone things and are inefficient.'

Therefore, in order to be happy, efficient management of time is a must. The most difficult task can be completed if a day-wise schedule is prepared and strict adherence is ensured. As one advances in one's endeavour and meets deadlines, there emerges a great feeling of confidence, achievement and control over life. It leads to a rich sense of well-being and happiness, and contributes significantly to the positive attitude of a person.

If You Think, You Can

The third important element of happy people is the sense of optimism about life. People having a strong sense of optimism invariably enjoy better health and greater success in life. In *The Power of Positive Thinking*, Norman Vincent Peale says, 'If you think in negative terms, you will get negative results. If you think in positive terms, you will get positive results. That is the simple fact of an astonishing law of prosperity and success.'

Robert Shuler declares in *The Be-Happy Attitudes*: 'The good news is that the bad news can be turned into good news when you change your attitude.' About two thousand years ago, Virgil propounded the same concept in his *Aeneid*: 'They can because they think they can.'

Caution and Optimism

A person having a life-affirming attitude enjoys far more joy and vitality than a person who is a habitual pessimist. The basic recipe for happiness is a positive and balanced attitude towards life. Excessive positivism also gives false notions and needs to be avoided. One should use a proper mix of caution, optimism and determination as only such an attitude can lead to hope, enthusiasm and realism in life. Such a person will be able to face even the worst adversities.

Reinhold Niebuhr echoes the same wisdom in his *Serenity Prayer*:

> God grant me the serenity
> to accept the things I cannot change,
> courage to change the things I can,
> and wisdom to know the difference.

Extroverts Enjoy Greater Happiness

The fourth most important element of personality is the quality of being extrovert. It is observed that extroverts enjoy greater happiness and lead a much more rewarding life. They are generally more comfortable in meeting people, even strangers get adequate attention from them. Extroverts are very quick to relate with others. They get easily involved with social groups, and have a larger and better circle of friends and acquaintances. Consequently, they enjoy better social support and get affection and respect from all quarters. Happiness depends upon our sense of self-esteem, control over life, optimism and the willingness to socialize.

Architects of Our Future

It is pertinent to ask whether we can drop the negative aspects of our personality and feel happiness by conscious effort. One school of thought believes that heredity influences and shapes our personalities. This may be true to a large extent, but there is absolutely no doubt that we have the power to change our destiny and add new element to our personality by conscious effort.

In this reference, author David G. Myers says, 'It's also true that we have the power to affect our own destinies, for we are the creators as well as the creature of our social worlds. We may be products of our past, but we also are architects of our future.'

> **Learning Points:**
>
> - The best predictor of happiness in life is not wealth or income, friends, or family, but self-esteem.
> - Positive self-esteem is a great protection against anxiety and depression.
> - Those who are not able to fill their time with worthwhile activities are found to be unhappy and unstable by temperament.
> - Extroverts enjoy greater happiness and lead a much more rewarding life.
> - We have the power to change our destiny and acquire new elements in our personality by conscious effort.

Chapter 12

To Love and Be loved

'There is only one happiness in this life, to love and be loved.'

—George Sand, French novelist,
memoirist and journalist

If we go through the definition of love and its relationship with happiness, we find that people have variously defined the phenomenon of love, but the common thread is that love is a feeling universally acclaimed to be noble, exalted, divine and most sought after. It gives meaning to life and connects two souls in a simple, elevating and exciting but a complex relationship.

It is a phenomenon that merges the identity of two persons and produces a highly surcharged and enlightened chemistry between them. Poets, philosophers and thinkers have tried to define love in various ways, but it remains an enigma.

A State of Mind

There is no doubt that love is the most essential and important factor for happiness and that is why love dominates the psyche of kings as well as commoners, saints as well as mere mortals. Most works of art—whether poetry, painting, drama, fiction or epics—are generally based on the theme of love. The world of literature and entertainment revolves around the ecstasy of love.

Everybody on this earth yearns for love. People are willing to do anything for the sake of love. The most common elements in love include mutual understanding, ease and comfort in a loved one's company and willingness to be intimate and committed. In fact, it is a state of mind that makes the partners involved feel exalted, expansive and extremely joyful.

If You Love One, You Love All

Psychoanalyst Anthony Storrs says, 'All the world loves a lover, and a lover loves all the world.' If a person is in passionate love, the whole world seems extremely beautiful. Poetess and author Amrita Pritam echoes the same feelings when she says, 'If you love one, you love all. You love the whole world.'

There is absolutely no doubt that love is the fountainhead of genuine joy and happiness, but the thrill of the ecstasy, the 'walking together six inches above the ground' and 'floating on the cloud feeling', do not sustain for long even in the most passionate love relationships. Passion and excitement in love wane with time, and gradually a sense of boredom, indifference and intolerance creeps into relationships. It happens mostly in cultures and societies where there is too much emphasis on physical aspects of love, and mutual support, commitment and respect are accorded less priority.

A Union of Two Beings

Love is such a unique and complex feeling that everybody experiences it differently and relates to it in his or her own way, depending on their upbringing, experience and view of life. It encompasses the feelings of happiness, fulfilment and well-being. Love is characterized as a feeling of interdependence for happiness and meaning in life between two people.

Love touches the three most dominant aspects of a human being—intimacy, passion and commitment. Intimacy may lead to its ultimate elevation, where two beings merge their identity into one and realize the ultimate bliss. This is the highest potential and the possibility of love. But this extreme is rarely achieved.

Commitment, a Conscious Decision

Passionate feelings deal with externalities and physiological aspects of the lovers and provide charge and energy to sustain and maintain the relationship. But quite often 'the law of diminishing returns' starts operating even in this relationship, and passion and excitement lessen. Commitment is a conscious decision on both sides to accept each other and trust and strengthen the feeling of love on a regular basis. Love is a golden mix of the above elements and its edifice stands on the strength of these pillars.

Love Has Many Shades

Everybody yearns for attention, commitment and love. People live for love and even die for it. There is strong element of love and affection in many other close relationships as well. The bond between parents and children, spouses, close relatives and intimate friends are extremely exalted where concerns for each other's happiness and well-being are uppermost. These feelings of trust, understanding, concern, ease and comfort in the company of loved ones are common to love relationships.

However, some elements of human feelings and behaviour are quite distinct in love. In love, often the partners involved are immensely keen to express their longings physically and have a very strong desire to keep the relationship exclusive. In addition, intense fascination, mutual admiration and a sense of possessiveness are other dominant feelings in this relationship.

The substance of love has been beautifully summarized by Kahlil Gibran in his poem 'On Love' in his magnum opus *The Prophet*:

> When love beckons to you, follow him,
> Though his ways are hard and steep
> And when his wings enfold you, yield to him,
> Though the sword hidden among his pinions,
> may wound you.
> Love gives naught but itself and takes naught but from itself.
> Love possesses not, nor would it be possessed;
> For love is sufficient unto love.

Learning Points:

- There is only one happiness in this life—to love and be loved.
- It is a state of mind, which makes the partners involved feel exalted, expansive and extremely joyful.
- Love gives meaning to life and connects two souls in a most simple, elevating and exciting relationship.
- Love touches the three most dominant aspects of a human being—intimacy, passion and commitment.

Chapter 13

The Need of a Soulmate

'There is no more lovely, friendly and charming relationship, communion or company than a good marriage.'

—Martin Luther, German theologian, professor and church reformer

Marriage is an important institution and married people are found to be happier with life as compared to those who are unmarried. However, it is not true to say that marriage is a necessary and sufficient condition for happiness in life.

There are logical reasons to make one feel happy in marriage. Marriage provides a new role to a person as one becomes a life partner of someone to whom one becomes deeply attached. Once children are born, it leads to another new role of parenthood. Parenthood offers novel opportunities to partners and gives them a joy and thrill that is difficult to compare with any other achievement.

Despite all the joy and happiness attached with marriage, no other institution faces more problems and challenges than marriage. Census data of the US and Canada have revealed that about 50 per cent of the marriages in the US and 40 per cent in Canada invariably end in divorce. This phenomenon is now not uncommon in India either.

Performs a Vital Role

Marriage performs a vital role, as it regulates family life and ensures proper succession and inheritance in society. It gives sanctity and stability to the family and ultimately to society. The institution of marriage is one of the most basic and exalted ones. However, the recent trend of 'living-in' without getting married is also catching the fancy of many people in urban areas across the world. In my opinion, this concept, in a way, is a blatant negation of the institution of marriage.

Threats to the Institution of Marriage

Another challenge to the institution of marriage is the emerging trend of single motherhood despite safe birth control measures and legalization of abortion in most parts of the world.

There is a widespread feeling that 'live-in' partners enjoy closer and more intimate bonding than married couples. This assumption could be because partners in a live-in relationship consciously come together with a greater willingness to share and support each other equally. In many cases, it is a testing ground for partners to assess the willingness and suitability to opt for a lifelong relationship of wedlock.

No End to Human Lust

There being no end to the vagaries of human lust and permissiveness, all is not well even in 'live-in' relationships. As compared to the marriages where 'live-in' was not involved, 'live-in' relationships had a higher rate of separation.* It may be because people who take the decision of living together out of wedlock are already less committed to the concept of pair-bonding.

No Certainty of Happiness

There is no certainty that marriage will lead to happiness. It depends on the upbringing of the partners, expectations from the relationship and the willingness to accommodate each other. There is no definite formula to ensure happiness in married life. However, couples with a keen willingness to accommodate each other in day-to-day scenarios may have better chances at prolonging their relationship. In addition, couples having stable income, good education and spiritual leanings may enjoy more happiness and satisfaction in marriage. But there are no conclusive evidences to suggest that the above factors will definitely lead to a happy marriage.

Sociologists have been working hard to find out the major ingredients of a happy marriage. Many couples enjoy warmth and comfort in marriage throughout their lives,

---

*Stanley, Scott M., and Galena K. Rhoades, *What's the Plan? Cohabitation, Engagement, and Divorce*, Institute for Family Studies, 2023, p. 4, https://tinyurl.com/wmp6t4ch. Accessed on 31 August 2023.

whereas others start feeling trapped, and suffer pain, hurt and alienation.

A Soulmate

Marriage is a very important factor in the matrix of happiness. A successful marriage depends on a couple's overall satisfaction from togetherness, their social and financial achievements and the dominant social and cultural trends of the times and the society they belong to. The most decisive factor for the overall quality of married life and resulting happiness is the effort both spouses put into being a soulmate for each other and true sharers of whatever comes their way in the passage of life.

Sharing Is the Key

Another important factor for a happy and successful marriage is the sense of sharing between both the partners. Wherever this is lacking, there is bound to be distress and agony. The domination of one partner over the other creates conflict and irritation in marriage . The feeling of sharing as equal partners is the key to happiness. It needs conscious effort of both the partners to make it work by being available to each other, and be genuinely willing to share the ups and downs of life. The partners should be sensitive to the views, dreams and desires of each other, and should be open to frankly discuss issues and sort out differences and disagreements arising in the course of life. The bedrock of marriage is trust, mutual understanding, honest communication and sharing.

A Happy Marriage

It is a common observation that between couples the occasions to agree, approve and laugh together far outnumber the occasions to disagree, criticize and dominate. The cardinal principle for a happy married life is the willingness of partners to be sensitive in their speech and conduct and make efforts to enhance the love and warmth of the relationship on a regular basis. In the absence of such efforts, marriages tend to decay and become stale. Likewise, the maxim that 'familiarity breeds contempt' also operates in the institution of marriage. There should be adequate opportunity for both the spouses to discuss and disagree. Mutual respect, understanding and willingness to co-operate are essential ingredients for a happy marriage.

Mutual Love and Affection

A healthy and emotional bond is the bedrock of a solid, stable and enduring marriage. Emotional and physical aspects of a relationship work together, and simultaneously affect and strengthen the bond between the partners. There is no doubt that the lack of a physical relationship makes married life boring, loveless and irritating.

Another related aspect in the realm of physical relationship versus happiness is the question of warmth and quality of this relationship. In this debate, the quality aspect has the upper hand, as the physical relationship becomes much more joyful if there is closeness and warmth between the partners.

Spaces in Togetherness

The institution of marriage is very important for peace, prosperity and happiness in society, as children born and brought up in a joyful and successful marriage are found to be kind and responsible parents themselves. This cycle goes on and enriches society, which leads to the evolution of a developed culture and civilization.

Kahlil Gibran beautifully emphasizes the importance of space in marriage in his poem 'On Marriage' in his famous book *The Prophet*:

> But let there be spaces in your togetherness,
> And let the winds of the heavens dance
> between you.
> Love one another, but make not a bond
> of love:
> Let it rather be a moving sea between
> the shores of your souls.

Learning Points:

- Marriage is an important institution and married people are found to be happier in life.
- Marriage gives sanctity and stability to the family and ultimately to society.
- The feeling of sharing as equal partners is the key to happiness.
- The cardinal principle for a happy marriage is the willingness of partners to be sensitive in their thoughts, speech and conduct.
- There should be spaces in the togetherness of partners.

Chapter 14

The Greatest Wealth

'Health is a state of complete harmony of the body, mind and spirit. When one is free from physical disabilities and mental distractions, the gates of the soul open.'

—B.K.S. Iyengar, yogi and founder of Iyengar Yoga

Health is the greatest wealth. There is nothing more important than good health. Maintaining good health, both physical and mental, should be the top priority for everyone. It is said that a perfect body with sound mind is the greatest hope of human race. It is one's moral duty as well as basic need to be healthy in order to enjoy material as well as spiritual life and contribute to society.

Sound Health Is a Must

The objective of life is to be happy and content. All efforts and duties are performed for attaining happiness. To make these efforts, a sound body with an alert and creative mind is needed, as it is the means, the medium and the equipment for living. If we are not healthy, all the riches, power and position are useless and meaningless. A perfect body with sound health is a must for routine chores as well as creative accomplishments. Health is the basis of all social virtues. We are of no use to family or society if we are not healthy.

Food for a Sound Body

Food is said to have a direct link with human conduct and behaviour. The Bhagavad Gita says that the intent and conduct of a person largely depend on his choice of food. It even goes on to describe three kinds of food and correspondingly three kinds of persons. One can, to a certain degree, understand the nature and conduct of a person by knowing their food preferences.

Health and behaviour are interrelated aspects of human life. It has been the dominant belief through ages that by changing diet, thought and conduct, a human being can change oneself. It is mentioned in the Upanishads, 'As is the food, so is the mind.' Therefore, one should eat nourishing and agreeable food as the food not only affects one's health but also one's thoughts and conduct.

Physical Activity

Another important factor that positively affects our health is exercise and proper upkeep of the human body. In ancient times, not much emphasis was given to physical exercise, as before the era of industrialization almost everybody had to do a fair amount of physical work as part of life's routine. However, over the last two centuries, the trend of our civilization has been to avoid physical exercise and reduce labour-intensive activities. Today, we hardly exert ourselves in performing any of the chores from morning till night. We have almost forgotten that we need physical activity for health and happiness.

With the increasing number of labour-saving devices, physical activity has been reduced to such an extent that a person hardly ever perspires. In the sweat-drenched, labour-intensive era of the past, keeping fit and staying in shape was not an issue; in today's jet-set lifestyle, keeping fit and being physically active has acquired tremendous importance in our lives.

Sedentary Lifestyle

Today, a person spends a greater part of their life either sitting or lying down—be it at home, in the car, at functions or while watching television. This sedentary lifestyle has ushered in an era of obesity, as the old energy-balance equation of 'calories in—calories out' has been thrown out of gear. On top of this, there is no discipline on food intake. Junk food has become very popular and people usually have no time for any physical activity.

Affluent societies today face two major challenges that are affecting human health as well as the quality of life. The first is the phenomenon of obesity and the other is a prevalent tendency to avoid any kind of physical activity. Both have a cause-and-effect relationship with each other and need to be tackled on priority.

Exercise Works Wonders

Exercise is very crucial for our health, as it works wonders for the heart by improving lipid profile, reducing the risk of heart-diseases, and enhancing overall vitality and immunity. It helps in strengthening bones for all age-groups and is immensely helpful in maintaining proper blood pressure. It reduces the chances of hypertension, anxiety and depression. It also improves cognitive functions in one's senior years. Fitness is not a matter of being skinny. It is a matter of being healthy, taking into consideration all the health parameters.

Regular Physical Activity

It is medically proven that after a person crosses the age of 25, the body experiences decay at the rate of about 1 per cent a year in terms of physical fitness. It is estimated that a good walking regime may improve overall physical health up to 15 per cent in just three months.

In fact, to ensure physical fitness, one of the easier options is to adopt a physical activity-oriented lifestyle as a part of daily routine. We can introduce elements of physical activity in our daily chores. Some such activities are listed below:

- Park the vehicle at a distance and walk to the destination.
- Use steps and staircases instead of an elevator.
- Walk down to meet a friend or a colleague instead of using the phone or e-mail.
- Take a walk down the corridor to receive or see off people.
- Share household chores with family members whenever possible.
- Develop a habit of pre-dinner or post-dinner walk.

- Actively participate in community services involving physical activities.

Making these activities a part of our daily routine can be helpful in improving heart and respiratory fitness, muscular strength and reducing body fat.

Exercise All Seven Days

To ensure a significant improvement in physical fitness and to lose weight in accordance with a definite time schedule, a vigorous exercise regime is needed. The duration of these exercises should be a minimum of 30–45 minutes, depending upon one's physical condition and need. But these exercises need to be done all seven days of the week.

Some of the exercises that are strongly recommended are:

- Aerobic exercises, such as walking, jogging, cycling and swimming, involve the use of large muscles in rhythmic motion, improving cardiovascular conditioning.
- Strength training exercises such as weightlifting improves muscular strength and endurance, and helps in bone density and metabolism.
- Stretching exercises involving slow and gentle movement elongates the body muscles and improve flexibility of the body.
- Yogic exercises, like asanas, pranayama and meditation, improve fitness, flexibility and immunity of the body. Yoga is the finest exercise and has been practised for thousands of years. It increases flexibility, strength, balance and range of motion in addition to reducing stress and anxiety.
- The exercises may be done at one stretch or in a staggered

manner. For best results, a 30-minute yoga session in the morning and a 30–45-minute walk in the evening will keep anybody healthy and happy.
- A brisk walk is the most popular aerobic exercise. Walking at a swift pace burns almost as many calories as running or jogging for the same distance. On an average, maintaining a walking pace of about 3.5 kilometres in 30 minutes is good for physical fitness.

No Blessing Is Greater

A healthy diet and physical activity are a must for keeping fit and healthy. It is a common observation that our thoughts and feelings greatly influence our health and behaviour. Positive thoughts, faith in God and human goodness make us energetic and vibrant, whereas self-doubt and worries make our life dull and drab.

A proper diet and regular exercise can make anybody healthy and happy. No blessing is greater than being healthy with an alert mind and positive attitude.

Learning Points:

- Good health is the most important asset for a person.
- As is the food, so is the mind.
- Regular exercise reduces the chances of hypertension, anxiety and depression.
- It also improves cognitive function in seniors.
- The right food and regular exercise can make anybody healthy and happy.

Chapter 15

Enjoy Every Moment

'Always hold fast to the present. Every situation, indeed every moment, is of infinite value, for it is the representative of a whole eternity.'

—Johann Wolfgang von Goethe,
German poet and playwright

If a person talks about misery, sorrows and stress in their life, everybody believes them, but if they say they are very happy, nobody is prepared to take them seriously. It sounds quite unbelievable to most people. After extensive research involving thousands of people and having observed their minds, Austrian neurologist and the founder of psychoanalysis, Sigmund Freud, had observed that man was incapable of happiness. That happiness is a fiction and that human beings can never be happy.

While Freud's statement appears to be overly pessimistic, the fact remains that most people sound unhappy most of the time. Very few people acknowledge cheerfully that they are happy and content with life. It is also true that of all the species on this planet, human beings are the only ones who can exercise choice regarding being happy or otherwise.

Happiness Depends on Us

Human beings are endowed with consciousness, a unique capability that other species have not been blessed with. Other species of flora and fauna have a definite life cycle of birth, ageing, decay and death, which are ordained by existence, and not much can be done by these species themselves. But it is not so with human beings, as they occupy a unique position and are endowed with the capability to create their own world and master their destiny.

It appears that something went wrong in the evolution of human beings as they learnt to be unhappy and miserable even on the slightest pretext. Our view of life determines our perceptions regarding the quality of our life. If we ponder on the issue, we conclude that our happiness depends entirely on us.

An Endless Race

In the initial phases of civilization, people lived in perfect harmony with nature; the pace of life being slow and free of anxiety, even minor achievements and festivals were occasions of great joy and celebration. With the passage of time, human life became complicated and it increasingly lost touch with nature. People became adept at searching for reasons to be sad and unhappy. However, the uppermost objective of human life has been to seek happiness for themselves and their near and dear ones.

In the present context, we all are seeking happiness in wealth, power, prestige and recognition. These are ever-expanding and unending avenues and get us nowhere.

In the process, we have discarded the intrinsic values of life that add meaning and make life happy and joyful. Pursuit of happiness through material objects and means of comfort is an endless race. It has made our life extremely competitive, as no amount of achievement in terms of prosperity, power and position is enough to make us happy for long.

The quest for joy has become an object of dreams, poetry and fantasy. It is difficult to find people discussing their happiness. But if we observe people describing their agony, there is discernible pleasure, even a gleam in their eyes. People often tend to exaggerate their sufferings and thus perpetuate negative feelings, which sets a vicious cycle in motion.

We Choose to Be Unhappy

We choose our reasons and logic to be unhappy and do not focus on the blessings of life. There is so much in life to be happy and grateful for. Having good health, being blessed with a loving life partner and obedient children should be an important reason to be happy and content in life. Likewise, viewing the magic of sunrise and sunset, a moonlit sky and varied colours of flowers in a garden should be enough to make us happy and joyful. But we have made our life so complicated that we have forgotten to relate with nature and its wonders. A human being can weave a complex web of desires, envy and intrigues to make themselves and everybody they know thoroughly unhappy and miserable.

Flow with Life

What is needed for happiness is a life-affirming attitude, an attitude of joy and celebration. Enjoying every moment of living and celebrating the gifts of life should be of prime importance, but unfortunately it's not so. The mad rush for wealth, prestige and position never permits us to pause and think about what all we have, and thus prohibits us from enjoying life with family and friends. The thirst for more—more than the neighbours, more than the colleagues or even more than one's sibling or a family member—keeps us restless and unhappy.

The various aspects of nature and the seasons should be enough to keep us happy and thrilled but due to our distorted views of life, we never find time to derive joy from its grandeur. The basic point in the matrix of happiness is to be willing and ready to embrace life and flow with it. To be joyful and happy, one must change one's view of life and expectations from it.

Pleasure Is Momentary

Happiness depends on the level and direction of our consciousness. To a person in search of riches, comfort and luxury, pleasure is all that matters. Pleasure may be defined as a feeling, an experience of satisfaction, enjoyment and perceived happiness through the sense organs. The fact remains that the body can experience only fleeting sensations, as the pleasure obtained from having good food, smelling a fragrance, listening to good music, watching a pleasant sight or experiencing a desirable touch, etc., are momentary in nature. To call such momentary and fleeting experiences as happiness does not appear to be proper. Some scholars call this feeling a diversion, a temporary escape from the routine and mundane life.

Meaning in Life

Serious contemplation reveals that genuine happiness should not be momentary or fleeting. It should not depend on wealth, prestige and power. Happiness is person-specific, something concerned with one's feelings. But in the present context of time, people consider ego satisfaction and sensory feelings to be the decisive elements of happiness. Most people spend their lives going from one sensation to another and expend immense resource and energy for momentary thrills of life. In fact, they lead superficial lives devoid of any depth and meaning.

This kind of life provides momentary distraction from a monotonous routine but there is a quick relapse into the same old groove and the same old unhappiness. A change of diet, wearing costly clothes, a big house and costly cars, etc., never give anybody any real happiness. This kind of life may provide ego satisfaction and fleeting pleasure for some time but adds no worth or meaning to life.

Sensual pleasure can never lead to genuine and lasting happiness. To realize genuine happiness, one must work for a life of meaning and substance. For an enriched life, a person needs some inclination towards art, culture, music and other finer aspects of life. Gradually, such a person begins enjoying these activities and can appreciate the beauty and splendour much better when compared to a person pursuing mundane sensual pleasures.

Happiness Is a By-Product

Happiness is not a direct product of an act or pursuit. It is a by-product of our thoughts, actions and philosophy of life. Winning the Nobel Prize, the birth of a long-desired child or climbing Mount Everest may not make a person happy for long, though such achievements do result in great joy and happiness for the time being. After some time, even such major achievements cease to provide any thrill, and life relapses into the same old pattern.

Happiness on a sustained basis does not lie in great achievements. It is a result of regular efforts, incremental steps towards one's goals, a sense of kindness and the ability to accommodate and take people along by being large-hearted. The secret of happiness lies in sharing the joys and sorrows of others without any expectations for doing so.

A Calm and Quiet Life

The life of the Buddha offers a great example of comfort and worldly pleasures not bringing genuine happiness. Prince Siddhartha left his family and kingdom, and met various learned teachers, scholars and renowned saints and sages. He also practised severe penance but his mind remained agitated and far from peace. Peace descended on him only when he deserted all his efforts and reflected within. The freedom from efforts led to his awakening, and the peace he had sought for so long finally dawned on him. Ultimately, Prince Siddhartha became the Buddha, the Enlightened One.

The essence of happiness is to lead a calm and quiet life, develop harmony with nature and try to enjoy every moment as it comes. Ego and envy are the greatest hindrances as they lead us nowhere and are the biggest roadblock in the journey to happiness.

Be with Yourself

There is an interesting story about Russian novelist Maxim Gorky's visit to America. He was shown all the important tourist spots and centres of entertainment. As the tour progressed, Gorky appeared progressively sad and disappointed. The organizers were worried and the guide had to ask Gorky for the reason. He replied that he was feeling very sad and disillusioned, as America appeared to have become such a dull place that people needed so many tourist spots and means of entertainment. Only those people who are joyless and empty from within take recourse to external means of entertainment. The greatest contentment lies in being what one really is.

The practice of deep contemplation about our thoughts, beliefs, intentions, desires and goals is a must for happiness. We need to identify the factors that make us feel elevated and joyful, and act accordingly.

Be Ready for It

Happiness in life lies in the most simple and basic things. Physical well-being is very closely related with emotional well-being. Happiness does not depend on what we have but is a function of our personal growth, that is, what we really are from within and are striving to be. To be happy, we need to be ourselves, and be willing to flow with the current of life.

Thoughts of the past and future make us restless and hamper our journey on the path of happiness. Nothing has ever been achieved in the past, nor can it be achieved in the future as all our acts, deeds and achievements happen in the present moment. We can only retrospect and analyse our past acts, and, at the most, dream and plan our future. Therefore, for joyful living, we should be focussed on what is here and now, and try to live every moment to its fullest possibility.

Learning Points:

- Very few people acknowledge that they are happy and content with life.
- Our happiness depends entirely on us.
- We failingly seek happiness in wealth, power, prestige and recognition.
- We choose our reasons to be unhappy and do not focus on the blessings of life.
- There is so much in life to be happy and grateful for.

Chapter 16

Duty of Being Happy

'The happiest life is that which constantly exercises and educates what is best in us.'

—Philip Gilbert Hamerton, English artist

The pursuit of happiness is one of the basic reasons for all our acts and endeavours. It is a considered decision and a conscious choice. The duty of being happy is one of the most important aspects of our life, but most of us run after wealth, prestige and power. We generally do not pause to ponder about what really gives us happiness. It is a common belief that accumulation of luxury objects and other material things will give us happiness. A serious contemplation of our life will tell us that this is a false belief.

Happiness Is Contagious

In simple words, happiness is a state of being happy, vibrant and upbeat. Happiness is also contagious. A person of happy disposition affects the mood and psyche of anyone they meet. The position or status of a person does not matter much in their way of interaction with people. A happy person is generally sweet, warm and nice to all. On the other hand, a person with a sad and gloomy nature spreads dreary and sombre vibes wherever they go. Such a person's despondent vibrations repel people irrespective of their wealth and status.

Wired from Within

Human beings are wired from within to seek cheer and joy, and be attracted to people who are happy and affable by nature. People bursting with joy attract many friends and colleagues, as they are a source of happiness. Such people experience great success in life and are quite fun to be with. They are friendly by nature and ever willing to help people by sharing in their grief and suffering.

Gifts of Life

The cardinal principle to be happy in life is to understand that nothing in life should be taken for granted. What is needed in life is the 'attitude to live and let live'. Everybody wants to enjoy life and be happy, but most people magnify the reverses and deprivations of life, and rarely focus on the blessings of life. To be happy, we should be aware of the gifts of life that have been bestowed on us by family and destiny. The habit of comparing ourselves with those who are in a better and privileged position is the root cause of unhappiness.

Never Be Self-Centred

Another cause of unhappiness is being self-centred and paying no attention to others. If good things happen to us or our family, we feel extremely joyful, but on the promotion and success of our colleagues and neighbours, we do not feel joy and rather feel jealous and unhappy. This is the major cause of unhappiness in life. This feeling of differentiation operates at all levels and becomes strongly ingrained in our psyche.

Expand Your Consciousness

The secret of happiness lies in expanding our consciousness beyond the limits of family, caste, community, gender, etc., and feel one with humanity. Our scriptures speak of seeing the whole world as a family. The phrase *Vasudhaiva Kutumbakam* has been extolled in the Vedas and followed in many other scriptures. We need to imbibe this philosophy to make everyone's life joyful and make the world a better place.

> *Ayam nijah paroveti ganana laghuchetasam,*
> *udaracharitanantu vasudhaiva kutumbakam*
>
> [One is our own, the other a stranger, think the small minded.
> For the magnanimous, the entire world is a family.]
>
> —Maha Upanishad VI. 71–73

Learning Points:

- We do not pause to ponder about what really gives us happiness.
- Happiness is a state of being happy, vibrant and upbeat.
- A happy person is generally sweet, warm and nice to all.
- The secret of happiness lies in feeling one with humanity.
- The habit of comparing ourselves with others is the root cause of unhappiness.

Chapter 17

The Purpose of Life

'The purpose of life is not to be happy. It is to be useful, to be honorable, to be compassionate, to have it make some difference that you have lived and lived well.'

—Ralph Waldo Emerson, American essayist, abolitionist and philosopher

It is said that successful people don't try to change the wind, they reset their sails. Success in life depends upon how much we understand ourselves, what we value most and are willing to devote time, effort and energy to, and our ability to understand our strengths and weaknesses.

An Enthusiastic Approach

Giving due priority to one's purpose and working hard towards that purpose is very important to lead a happy and successful life. The most important aspect of happy people is their enthusiasm and passion for work. The way they walk, talk and attend to the most trivial and ordinary chores of life indicates their passion and enthusiasm. The American thinker Ralph Waldo Emerson said, 'Nothing great was ever achieved without enthusiasm.'

Enthusiasm for work is something that comes from within. It is a part of the personality of successful and happy people. One cannot be trained to be enthusiastic, though positive stimuli and success can motivate people enormously. A person having vision and capacity to take risks is sure to make their life successful. The path of success and happiness is quite rugged and uneven, and needs intelligent use of intuition, drive and energy to sustain the journey.

No Shortcut to Happiness

The science and philosophy of happiness can be quite complex, and differ from person to person. There is no universal formula for happiness. Ordinarily, happiness is equated with wealth, power and position in society, but these factors in themselves are never adequate to ensure happiness. Balance in life, a friendly and loving spouse, understanding parents, obedient children, close family ties, sound health, creativity, spirituality and enthusiasm are other factors that make life wholesome, happy and meaningful. The effort to achieve success and happiness is not a one-day affair or one-time exercise. It is a process, a habit, a continuous journey.

Success Is Not Enough

On the face of it, success and happiness appear to be cause-and-effect, but serious contemplation reveals that while success and happiness can travel together, they need not be mutually dependent. One success may lead to another and drive the doer on the path of endless striving without any ultimate destination. Can such a journey really lead to happiness? The chain reaction of effort and success can lead to a state of mind where one gets fully immersed within oneself. Such a state of mind can never lead to happiness, although it may lead to a series of successes. Therefore, success does make a person happy for some time, but happiness on a regular basis will have to be sought elsewhere.

There is no consensus about what constitutes success, but it is certain that an honest sense of purpose, perseverance, energy, enthusiasm and pragmatic use of time and resources will ensure success in life. Likewise, a balanced and value-based life, investment in relationships and pursuit of right causes are the factors responsible for a happy and meaningful life.

Matter of Decision

Happiness in life is largely a matter of decision and effort. To be happy, one should make the right moves and adequate efforts. Life is a game and we must learn to achieve results practise and follow the rules, use proper tactics and revise our roadmap from time to time. Life is nothing but a sequence of outcomes of the decisions we make and the efforts we put in. Our decisions and actions largely determine the content and substance of our life. One's choice of friends, the educational institutions one ends up in, the profession one partakes in, the life partner one chooses, along with habits and choices such as abstaining from drugs and smoking, and having a pleasing disposition—such factors affect the quality of our life and determine our happiness in the long run.

The Need to Dream

Lord Richard Layard, a professor at the London School of Economics and a leading researcher on happiness, says, 'Happiness is a balance between your expectations and your attainments. One way is to get what you want. The other is liking what you get.'

We need to have a dream that drives us to be happy on a sustainable basis. Mere possessions and pursuit of thrill cannot sustain happiness for long. Those who have some lofty dream with a definite roadmap and sincerely strive to achieve this will always find reasons to be happy.

Make the World a Better Place

The progress in culture and civilization in the world is a result of the sustained effort of generations who followed their dreams and did their best in making the world a better place than the one they had found.

It really does not matter how much time one spends on earth, how much name and fame one acquires or how much wealth is accumulated. What matters is the number of positive vibrations a person can radiate and the number of lives they are able to touch and affect in a positive manner. In brief, the purpose of life is to be of some value, service and use to others, and contribute in some way in making things better.

Learning Points:

- Successful people don't try to change the wind, they reset their sails.
- The most important aspect of happy people is their enthusiasm and passion.
- Nothing great was ever achieved without enthusiasm.
- There is no universal formula for happiness.
- To be happy, one should make adequate efforts.

Chapter 18

Be Your Best

'The happiness that is genuinely satisfying is accompanied by the fullest exercise of our faculties and the fullest realization of the world in which we live.'

—Bertrand Russell, British mathematician

The concept of happiness and its significance has been uppermost in the minds of laymen as well as the learned for ages. Happiness has been the most important goal of human life. Aristotle called it *summum bonum*, the 'chief good' for the human being. We desire wealth, prestige and power because we believe that the possession of these will make us happy. The question remains whether material goods really lead to happiness.

Expectations Determine Happiness

The human brain has a specific area that determines the expectation of a material possession. And as soon as the material goal is achieved, the brain recalibrates the expectation levels. This means that if expectations are high, a person could be unhappy despite having achieved success, whereas another person may be exceedingly happy if their achievement—even though smaller—exceeded their expectation.

Brain scans have shown that the human brain has a 'fairness' switch. We may get a lot of things in life but if we think it was not equitable and fair, we experience unhappiness. Likewise, if we realize that we have been treated fairly, we feel great even if very little falls to our fate.

Hierarchy of Needs

Abraham Harold Maslow, the American psychologist, established the pyramidical model of the hierarchy of needs, placing material needs at the bottom and self-actualization at the top. Including the basic needs of air, water and food, he described five broader layers of needs.

Physiological needs

Physiological needs are needs related to our physical survival and include the need for oxygen, water, protein, salt, sugar, calcium, other minerals and vitamins, etc. In addition, one needs to be active, take rest, sleep, release waste, avoid pain and satisfy the need for sex.

Need for safety and security

When physiological needs are met, the second level of needs crave to be satiated. One becomes increasingly interested in finding a safe environment, stability and protection. These needs manifest themselves in the form of an urge for a comfortable house in a safe neighbourhood, job security and good career prospects.

Love and need to belong

Once the above two needs are taken care of, the third need is attention. One begins to feel the need for friends, family and affectionate relationships. These needs are exhibited in our desire to love, marry, raise a family and be a part of a greater community or a larger group.

Esteem needs

After physiological needs, the need for safety and security, and the need for love and belongingness are met, the need for esteem comes to the fore. According to Maslow, there are two versions of esteem needs—a lower one and higher one. The lower one is the need for attention, recognition, status, fame, glory, reputation, appreciation and dignity. The higher form of esteem involves need for self-respect, confidence, competence, achievement and freedom.

The need for self-actualization

Abrahm Maslow believed that musicians must make the best music, artists must paint beautiful portraits and landscapes, and poets must write their best poems to be at peace. A person must grow to reach that stage they were meant to be. People should be true to their own nature and achieve to the best of their possibilities. Maslow called this need as self-actualization.

Deficit Needs

Maslow called the bottom four levels as 'deficit needs' or 'D-needs'. If one has a deficit of one need, one tries to fulfil that need. But if the above needs are fulfilled, one has a feeling of emptiness and worthlessness, as the above needs cease to be a motivating force. All these needs are essentially survival needs. Even love and esteem are needed for our health and happiness. These needs are built into us genetically, just like our instincts.

The upward journey from physiological needs to those that are higher in the hierarchy passes through various stages. The dominant needs of the newborn baby are physiological in nature, which later change to the urges of safety, security, attention, affection, etc. As one advances in age, the need for self-esteem acquires increased importance. Under stressful conditions or under threat of survival, people tend to 'regress' to a lower stage in the hierarchy of needs. Whenever there are upheavals in the life of a person, they crave attention and affection just like a child. Likewise, in the hour of tragedy, people crave love and care from various quarters.

These phenomena occur not only in the lives of human beings but in the life cycles of communities and societies as well. Whenever there is a national crisis, people start clamouring for strong leadership to set things right. Likewise, during natural calamities, such as floods and earthquakes, physiological needs of survivors assume prime importance. If we ask people about their view of life or their concept of an ideal life, we can analyse their pattern of needs and their circumstances.

Realizing Your Full Potential

Material gains offer happiness only up to a point that ensures survival and some social status. Thereafter, the need for safety and security and the urge to love and be loved takes over. Many individuals stop at this level and feel happy; others continue their journey to the next level of self-esteem and then to the ultimate human urge of self-actualization.

All of us have immense potential for growth and we carry different possible versions of ourselves hidden in our being. It depends upon us to awaken it or let it remain buried there. Most people opt for an easy and comfortable life rather than doing their best and realizing their full potential.

According to Maslow, 'Self-actualization is the intrinsic growth of what is already in the organism, or more accurately, of what the organism is.' He studied healthy people whereas most psychologists at his time studied sick people to draw their conclusions. He conducted his research for 20 years on people who had the tendency for 'full use and exploitation of their talents, capacities, potentialities'.

Self-Actualizing People

Self-actualizing persons have better perception of reality and are comfortable with it. Such persons are unthreatened by the unknown. They are logical, efficient and have superior ability to analyse and see the truth. Self-actualizing persons accept themselves, others and the world as it is. They understand human nature and enjoy their life without any guilt; they do not have unnecessary inhibitions.

Motivation for Growth

Self-actualizing persons are spontaneous in their thoughts and are motivated to strive for further growth. They focus on problems outside themselves and are mission oriented; their mission is the reason for their existence. They are serene, devoted to duty and do not bother about hurdles and worries. Self-actualizing persons retain their dignity and are willing to take responsibility. They tend to be alone, though they are not lonely. They are not deterred by personal misfortunes. Such people rely on their inner strength and are self-contained.

The most important characteristic of such people is their appreciation of basic goodness of life. They live the present moment to the fullest and their every moment is thrilling, transcending and spiritual.

Eight Ways to Self-Actualize

There are two processes necessary for self-actualization: self-exploration and self-action. The deeper the self-exploration, the closer one comes to self-actualization. There are eight ways to self-actualize:

i. Find out who you are, what you are, what you like and don't like, what is good and what is bad for you, where you are going and what is your mission.
ii. Experience things fully, vividly and selflessly. Throw yourself into experiencing things; concentrate entirely on the thing at hand and let it absorb you.
iii. Life is an ongoing process of choosing between safety and risk. Make growth your choice.
iv. Try to shut out external clues and let your experience

enable you to say what you truly feel.
v. Taking responsibility is self-actualizing. When in doubt, be honest. If you ponder deeply and are honest, you will take responsibility.
vi. Be prepared to be unpopular. Listen to your own likes and dislikes, and act accordingly.
vii. Use your intelligence and do the things you want to do well, no matter how insignificant these seem to be.
viii. Learn what you are good at and not so good at. Get rid of illusions and false notions.

Self-Actualized Life

This is the state when a person experiences a life that allows for optimal growth towards a better state of being. One becomes what one could be and achieves the best in one's chosen field.

It is only when a person can meet their basic needs that they can self-actualize. Psychotherapist Victor Frankl said that if one could find one's purpose in life, one could find one's happiness. All human beings are born with a unique set of aptitudes and most of us move from an emphasis on integration as found in childhood to an emphasis on uniqueness.

The basic tenets of self-actualization may be summarized as working hard at something that is joyous, that challenges our abilities, and is capable of rendering happiness to us. If tasks undertaken have a greater purpose and deeper meaning, we are on the path of self-actualization. It has the potential to usher us into a state of joy and bliss.

Learning Points:

- Abraham Harold Maslow established the pyramidical model of the hierarchy of needs, placing material needs at the bottom and self-actualization at the top.
- Once the needs of survival, safety and security, love and belonging, and esteem are fulfilled, one has a feeling of emptiness and worthlessness.
- Abraham Maslow believed that a person should grow to reach the stage they are meant to reach.
- Everybody should be true to their own nature and achieve their full potential.
- Self-actualization is working hard at something that is joyous, challenges our abilities and is capable of rendering happiness.

Chapter 19

A Matter of Choice

'Happiness is a choice, not a result. Nothing will make you happy until you choose to be happy.'

—Ralph Marston, American football player

We all want to be happy, but an honest observation reveals that none of us is willing to claim happiness. Happiness at its zenith is performing some great tasks, realizing some great purpose, or at least doing one's best in the pursuit of one's objectives. Happiness in general is being at peace with oneself and the world around. Happiness also means being free from fear, anxiety and worries.

Happiness entails being healthy, self-dependent and secure, imbuing the right attitudes, possessing the right view of life, and having good friends and an affectionate family. The right view of life does not simply mean having the right philosophical orientation. It means having a correct assessment of one's needs and capabilities, and adopting a balanced view and expectation towards life.

Make Others Happy

The common belief that fulfilling one's needs and desires will lead to happiness is not proved true in real life. Rather, it triggers a chain reaction and traps us in the web of ever-unsatisfied longings. The first step towards happiness must be taken by the individual, but the role of family and friends is also very crucial. The regulation of unbridled desires of the mind is a very important requirement for happiness. To be happy, the willingness to make others happy and give our best is of paramount importance. Getting into the habit of retrospection, or looking back into our conduct and motives, is another key to happiness.

Wealth Is Not Enough

The belief that happiness is based on accumulation of wealth and material objects or fulfilment of all the desires that crisscross our mind does not stand sincere scrutiny. Another popular notion that needs to be dispelled from our minds is that people who have faced tragedy can never be happy, or that poor and sick are bound to be unhappy. There are enough poor people who are happy despite their circumstances. There are also plenty of wealthy people who are thoroughly unhappy. Obviously, wealth or the lack of it does not have much to do with happiness.

Attitude and Response

Positive thoughts, good time management, good health, self-esteem, optimism, reliable friends, compatible life partner, proper rest, entertainment and, above all, some challenging assignments are factors that can lead to happiness. Our circumstances and environment are crucial factors in the matrix of happiness but what matters most is our attitude and response to the situations we face in life. Happiness depends hugely on our vision and philosophy. We need to develop a life-affirming attitude to be happy on a durable basis.

Another important aspect that affects happiness is the sense of discrimination between right and wrong, and between urgent and important tasks. We need to take full charge of the direction of our life and give due weightage to factors that may lead to genuine happiness. The false notion of carrying the burden of the world on our shoulders and the habit of worrying too much needs to be curbed.

Purpose in Life

In fact, being healthy and at peace with oneself and having some purpose in life is important for happiness. We need to shed the burden of ego and dedicate our life to making this world a better place to ensure joy and happiness. We may contribute towards improving ecology and environment, do something to bring a smile on the faces of the weary and tired, eradicate some evil in society or even educate our near and dear ones to be more caring, kind and considerate human beings.

Bear No Grudges

We should do our best to make our life comfortable and joyful. At the same time we should also be willing to face whatever comes our way without any undue excitement or grudge. The following Mother Goose rhyme beautifully affirms this attitude:

> For every ailment under the sun,
> There is a remedy, or there is none;
> If there is one, try to find it,
> If there be none, never mind it.

Find Your Anchor

Another important tool to realize happiness is to make a list of the issues worrying us, examine their importance and list the possible solutions. On closer scrutiny, we find that most of our worries are self-created and don't deserve serious contemplation, whereas some of the problems tackled properly can be turned into opportunities.

Life is full of struggles and there are bound to be ups and downs; to sail through life happily, we must find our own anchors that suit and enthuse us. It may be a hobby, prayer or meditation, or some other creative activity that engages our mind and gives us hope and courage during adverse moments of life.

Choosing Happiness

Happiness comes in various forms and manifestations. Getting love and affection from people around us, an agreeable environment, a calm and detached state of mind and a feeling of being in charge of our life invariably provide joy and happiness in life. Everything depends on our roadmap and willingness to revise it as and when needed.

To be happy on a sustainable basis, we should have a proper perspective of the situations we face, and a firm resolve to be true to our faith and conviction in the beauty and goodness of life. Ultimately, happiness is a matter of choice.

Learning Points:

- Happiness is being at peace with oneself and the world around.
- Happiness also means being free from fear, anxiety and worries.
- The willingness to make others happy and give our best is of paramount importance for happiness.
- The habit of retrospection is another key to happiness.

Chapter 20

Life Is Bliss

'The present moment is filled with joy and happiness. If you are attentive, you will see it.'

—Thich Nhat Hanh, Buddhist monk, peace activist and writer

The most important aspect of happiness is knowing 'happiness is a choice'. It may sound strange but quite often we do not choose happiness. Due to distorted notions and misplaced views of life, we create conditions that result in misery, anxiety and suffering. It's well known that waking up early and taking a morning walk are great for a happy beginning of the day, but due to the lack of motivation, many of us wake up late in the morning when the sun is high and the splendour of morning has subsided.

A Subjective Phenomenon

The simple definition of happiness is that happiness is a pleasant feeling about anything we come across in life. Taking rest when tired, drinking a glass of water when thirsty and listening to an old melody—all these create pleasant sensations in our mind. Our day-to-day experiences reveal that happiness is something totally dependent on the person concerned and their state of mind. In fact, happiness is a subjective phenomenon. A condition or situation that once caused happiness may bring unhappiness and misery at another time.

In fact, external objects, persons, places and situations only act as a stimulus. These stimuli affect our psyche, and depending upon our state of mind, we derive joy or sorrow. Thus, we are solely responsible for our happiness or otherwise. The love and affection, likes and dislikes, and successes and failures that we experience in life are all our own creations.

Perspective Matters

The cause of happiness lies in our own perceptions about the happenings of life. The feelings of joy or sorrow also depend upon our own perceptions and state of mind. According to sages and saints, the supreme goal of human life is to discriminate between the dualities of happiness and sorrows, and attain the state of supreme bliss. One who learns to control one's primordial feelings, overcoming all likes and dislikes, and detaches from the outer world is said to experience lasting joy.

In oriental theology, life is not a misery and the world around us is not a miserable place. Our perceptions about life and external conditions do bring sorrow and misery in life. Our ancient scriptures proclaim that life is not a misery but an eternal bliss. The Vedas say: 'From bliss did things come into being, in bliss do they exist, and to bliss do they return finally.'

As we advance in life, our perception of happiness also goes on evolving and acquiring new aspects. From the state of physical sensations (which may be called pleasure), one enters the realm of superior happiness that is joy (a higher level of perception). The highest level of happiness may be termed as bliss. Bliss is the perfect happiness, the complete joy, where nothing can be added or subtracted. Bliss is said to be the prime goal of human life.

The evolution of human life and the chance of attaining a higher degree of happiness is a question of individual choice and efforts. There are various schools of thought that prescribe various paths and means for happiness, but the basic theme is almost the same.

It Is in Our Hands

Ultimately, happiness is a decision, a simple matter of choice. This is highlighted by Linda Worley, professor of psychiatry at UAMS College of Medicine: 'Everyone deserves to be happy but for that to happen, there are some necessary ingredients including caring for our physical selves, taking control of our emotions, discovering and acting upon our true inner callings and value systems, and taking charge of the direction of our lives.'

She further adds, 'We need to realize that we have the ability to make difficult choice in our lives, the choices that will lead to happiness even though they may not please someone else. Many people base their happiness on pleasing others, as it feels good to receive external approvals. But that feeling is fleeting and does not last. It is very important to understand that we control the decisions we make. Whether or not we are happy depends upon us and no-one else.'

Things Happen for a Reason

Another key to happiness, according to Worley, is a concept called 'synchronicity'. Synchronicity is a meaningful coincidence supposedly meant to nudge a person towards a certain direction. In other words, it is a theory that says 'things happen in life for a reason'. The events happening in life can be converted into opportunities that take us further on the path of growth and development. Explaining this point, Worley further says, 'By following our dreams and paying attention to the "meaningful co-incidences" in life, we really can find the road to true happiness.'

One of the most important factors in the sphere of happiness is the role of value systems in human life. Often people do not put their best efforts and energy into the things they value most. People want their children to do exceedingly well in school, but they do not supervise them nor do they have the time to take feedback from the teachers concerned. Likewise, we all realize the importance of friendship to make life happy and enriching, but quite often we don't put efforts in making new friends or to renew contacts and invest time and attention into nurturing friendships.

Be Sensitive to Your Inner Voice

To ensure happiness, it is important to examine our value system and the factors that make us happy, and then make determined efforts to live accordingly. It is a matter of personal choice and decision to live according to that choice.

This is the key to achieving genuine happiness, joy or bliss, depending upon our choice and willingness.

We need to be sensitive to our inner voice in order to be happy. Happiness is not sustained through material acquisitions. It entirely depends on who we are and in what direction we are moving. To be happy, we need to listen to the wisdom of our body and the voice from within. While choosing a response, we should ask ourselves whether we are comfortable with it. If yes, we should move ahead.

Living In the Present

The habit of living in the present and shedding the baggage of the past is very basic to the feeling of happiness. The life of 'now' is the life of happiness. The tendency to identify ourselves with our mind needs to be curbed. We are not our mind, rather we possess intelligence beyond the mind, and that is supreme. We need to realize this fact. It will enable us to become the master of our mind, instead of becoming an obedient servant of the mind and its dictates.

Everybody has a distinctive personality, just as every human being is born with their own instincts and follows their own path depending upon their destiny and circumstances. The factors which make people happy differ from individual to individual and from situation to situation. Everybody must chart out their own roadmap for happiness, as it is a matter of choice, conviction and efforts.

Learning Points:

- The life of 'now' is the life of happiness.
- A situation that once caused happiness may bring unhappiness and misery at another time.
- As we advance in life, the perception of happiness also goes on evolving and acquiring new aspects.
- To be happy, we need to listen to the wisdom of our body and the voice from within.
- Happiness entirely depends on who we are and in what direction we are moving.

PART 3

CHOOSE HAPPINESS

Chapter 21

Treat Ups and Downs Alike

Yogasthah kurukarmani sangam tyaktvaa Dhananjaya.
Siddhyasiddhyoh samo bhutvaa samatvam yoga uchyate.

[O Arjuna! Perform your duties with equanimity, abandoning attachment;
being even-minded in success and failure is called yoga.]

—Bhagavad Gita 2.48

We must perform our actions with perfect calmness and composure and try to remain indifferent to the ensuing consequences. Acts performed with a stable mind without undue attachment and treating success and failure alike is called yoga in the Gita. The central theme of the Gita is maintaining equanimity and performing one's duty without any attachment. For success, one should act with perfect calmness, without bringing in personal inclinations and aversions. To be happy and joyful, a person should not only be able to control the agitations of their mind but also be able to transcend their own whims and fancies.

It does mean that one should perform one's duties in a disinterested manner. In fact, one should shun too much attachment to the act but continue to do his duties with focus and vigour. The secret of happiness is to do the task at hand with an attitude that takes life's happenings into its stride, and to never get swayed from one's chosen path. As seasons change in nature, life also has its ups and downs. Being overjoyed at success and depressed over failures does not take anybody far in life. Joy and suffering are an integral part of human life.

Attitude of Equanimity

The way to a happy life is to develop an attitude of equanimity and treat joy and suffering alike without being affected by them. But practising equanimity and transcending the dualities in life is easier said than done. The concept of yoga so well described in the Bhagavad Gita is nothing but the art of treating ups and downs of life in a calm and detatched manner. For a happy life, we should develop an attitude of equanimity and treat joy and suffering alike. In the Gita, Arjuna asks Krishna about the physical attributes of a person practising equanimity:

> *Sthitaprajnasya ka bhaashaa samaadhisthasya Keshava.*
> *Sthitdheeh kim prabhaasheta kimaaseeta vrajeta kim.*

[O Keshav! What is the disposition of one having stable mind and practising equanimity? How does one with a stable mind talk? How does he sit? How does he walk?]

—Bhagavad Gita 2.54

Conduct Reflects Innate Nature

In the aforementioned shloka, Arjuna asks about the characteristics of a person who has a stable mind, and wants to know the nature, intellect and the conduct of such a person. The conduct of a person is an expression of their thoughts and innate nature. If one is calm and quiet, one's way of behaving with people will be pleasant, calm and balanced. Likewise, the behaviour of a person with an agitated mind is bound to be erratic and unpredictable.

Krishna, responding to the question, describes the quality of such a person:

> *Prajahaati yadaa kaamaan sarvaanpaartha manogataan.*
> *Aatmanyevaatmanaa tushtah sthitprajnastadochyate.*
>
> [Arjuna, when one discards all desires of the mind and becomes satisfied in the self, he is said to be a *sthitprajna*, a person practising equanimity.]
>
> —Bhagavad Gita 2.55

The Outcome of Equanimity

A person practising equanimity renounces all their desires and remains content. The real test of equanimity is to have full control over one's desires and never allow it to affect one's peace of mind. It is a state of the mind in which a person is fully quiet and composed, and external forces never disturb their peace and calmness.

In day-to-day life, it is not easy to discard desires, but a person of stable mind will be able to take a balanced view of the happenings of life. A person with a sense of balance and practice in contemplation can exercise restraint on a free run of fancies and desires. Such a person can take good and bad happenings of life in their stride and live a happy and content life. According to the Bhagavad Gita, to be sthitprajna, a person of stable mind is to cast off all desires and become satisfied in one's own self. The real test is to discard all desires and then become such that desires are not able to affect one's peace of mind.

Learning Points:

- As seasons change in nature, life also has its ups and downs.
- Joy and suffering are integral part of human life.
- The concept of yoga in the Gita describes yoga as the art of treating ups and downs of life alike.

Chapter 22

Pleasure Is Desirable

'Pleasure is the only thing one should live for, nothing ages like happiness.'

—Oscar Wilde, Irish poet and playwright

Our happiness depends upon our own thoughts and deeds and the way we conduct ourselves. Most of us equate happiness with pleasure, wealth and position in society. There have been thinkers who consider pleasure to be the main objective of life. For a comfortable existence, these factors may be necessary, but they are not sufficient to make one happy.

Epicurus, an ancient Greek philosopher, advocated the importance of a simple life having minimum needs and some friends. He believed that knowledge should enable people to live a moral and spiritual life. He emphasized the significance of gut feeling and held it to be the real indicator of morality. According to him, one's gut feeling is more important than wisdom or precepts of scriptures.

Pleasure Is Desirable

Epicurus imparted great significance to pleasure and held that whatever gives pleasure is desirable and moral. He considered ataraxia to be the main objective of human life. Ataraxia is defined as calmness or peace of mind—an emotional tranquillity. He considered the state of tranquillity to be the highest kind of happiness. He also advocated the avoidance of pain to be the sole objective of human endeavour.

But, in real life situations, pain is necessary for higher gains. Discipline and exercise for good health, regular and focussed studies, hard work for success in career or business are obvious examples about the importance of taking pains in life.

Life without Anxiety

According to Epicurus, a life without anxiety, a habit of retrospection, faith in one's gut feeling and some good friends are needed for a happy and peaceful life. Retrospection enables a person to know themselves well and lead a purposeful life. The quality of life of a person does not depend so much on objects of luxury and comfort as on their view of life and control over desires and fancies.

Happiness is a function of basic life comforts, richness of thoughts, and presence of trustful, agreeable and amiable friends and relations.

Happiness as a Responsibility

The sum and substance of the Epicurean view of life is that happiness of a person is their own responsibility. External factors may affect life, but the ultimate consequences ensue from one's convictions, and the will to live in the light of one's own beliefs and guts. There is a prevalent belief that the main theme of the Epicurean way of life was 'eat, drink and be merry'. But many scholars hold that three things that he considered important for a happy life were friendship, freedom from anxiety and philosophical thinking. It is difficult to disagree with this conclusion even in the present.

Death Is Nothing

Epicurus' popularity lies in his philosophy of leading a simple life within limited means, acquiring experience and knowledge, and abstaining from pain and suffering. His thoughts on death also gave a sense of peace and relief to the people of his time. Epicurus propounded that there is nothing to fear in death. When a man dies, he feels nothing, as he is no longer there.

He famously said, 'Death is nothing to us.' When we exist, there is no death and when death occurs, we cease to exist. All sorts of feelings and consciousness are a part of life and end with death. Therefore, one should not fear death, as there is neither pain nor pleasure in death. The fear people have is the widespread belief that death is painful.

Learning Points:

- Knowledge should enable us to live a moral and spiritual life.
- Epicurus, an ancient Greek philosopher, held that whatever gives pleasure is desirable and moral.
- He believed that avoidance of pain is the sole objective of the human endeavour.

Chapter 23

Memory Stored in the Heart

'Gratitude is the wine for the soul. Go on. Get drunk.'

—Rumi, Persian poet and Sufi mystic

All of us need help from others to be happy and successful, as no one can act alone in conducting the business of life. But we hardly understand and appreciate the role of others in our life. Happiness is living every minute with love, grace and thankfulness. Thankfulness in a way is the beginning of feeling grateful.

Gratitude is a sincere acknowledgement of the assistance received from others in tangible or intangible form. Marcus Cicero, a great Roman statesman and philosopher, had said that gratitude is not only the greatest virtue but also the parent of all other virtues.

Gratitude Helps Us Grow

We take for granted the support and assistance of many people who truly deserve our sincere appreciation. Gratitude helps us to grow and spread happiness in our life and the lives of those around us. It is said that if we are grateful by nature, there is bound to be tremendous sweetness in our behaviour. Gratitude is an integral part of a happy existence. In fact, the root of happiness lies in being grateful and acknowledging all the help, support and inspiration we have received.

The Profoundness of Gratitude

It is a common observation that plants, flowers, trees, mountains, rivers, the moon and the stars all seem to be perfect in their beauty and dignity. As a sensitive viewer, one may find them to be joyful and be content in their existence. A feeling of gratitude reflects our basic goodness and introduces us to the beauty and grandeur of life.

Gratitude affects our thinking and conduct in a profound manner. It enriches our life and makes us calm and quiet. We can relate better not only with people around us but also our whole existence. Gratitude is a sign of a noble soul as nothing is more honourable than to accept the empathy and compassion of others and spread it around.

Gratitude Affects Our Health

There are many studies that prove that the feeling of gratitude has a profound effect on our health and happiness. It helps in reducing stress, anxiety and depression. The habit of gratitude has been found to be of paramount importance for those suffering from anxiety and sleeplessness. It is said to reduce the feelings of monotony, boredom and worthlessness. Gratitude is very strongly related to good health, happiness and a sense of well-being.

Gratitude Makes Us Virtuous

If we think seriously about the blessings of life and the role of various people in our life responsible in our growth and success, we are bound to feel grateful. If we express gratitude as a matter of habit in our day-to-day life, life becomes full of peace and harmony. Such a life gets transformed into a life of genuine love, kindness and prayer. We become full of empathy and compassion, and easily feel the pain, misery and suffering of others.

It opens an entirely new phase in life, as it not only makes us more acceptable and admired in the society but also makes us virtuous and our life full of purpose and meaning.

An Opportunity to Serve

Gratefulness is the best prayer and saves us from being selfish, haughty and egoistic. It makes us aware of the mystery of life and its fickleness. The attitude of gratitude spreads its own goodness and makes life an opportunity to serve and be useful to society. We should make conscious effort to ingrain this attitude in our psyche and make it an integral part of our life. It has great potential to make our life happy and blissful.

Learning Points:

- We hardly appreciate the role of others in our life.
- Gratitude is a sincere acknowledgement of the help and support received from others in tangible or intangible form.
- Gratitude is not only the greatest virtue but also the parent of all other virtues.

Chapter 24

Today Is the Best Day

'The future depends on what you do today.'

—Mahatma Gandhi, political ethicist and India's Father of the Nation

We should never postpone an activity that can be done today for the next day. We should make our best efforts to fully utilize the day. Benjamin Franklin said, 'You may delay, but time will not, and lost time is never found again.' We should take time in looking into pros and cons of a decision but once the call has been taken, we should never procrastinate. It is said that the only difference between success and failure is the will to act here and now.

Strike While the Iron's Hot

Most of us try to postpone action, especially in cases where the task at hand is risky and difficult. The secret of success lies in not only striking the iron while it is hot but also by striking it forcefully and repeatedly. It is true that we are not living in eternity and the time available is not endless. It should be our resolve to plan the day in advance and adhere to it scrupulously. Planning for any important activity should be done meticulously and no effort should be spared to complete it expeditiously. This is possible only when each person concerned acts with commitment and urgency, and performs tasks on a daily basis without falling into the trap of procrastination.

Today Is the Best Day

Life is made up of hours and days. A day wasted is a day lost forever. The old maxim that today is the best day and now is the right time holds true for all seasons and circumstances. Shakespeare rightly said that time and tide wait for none. Many of us lead an ordinary life simply because we failed to act on time and life bypassed us. Success in health, education and career depend on using each moment and each day in the best possible manner.

Action Is Better than Inaction

In many societies, there are superstitions regarding some days being more auspicious than others. Many people start a new project or take an important decision only on an auspicious day. Such tendencies should be curbed, as all days are equally crucial, and success ultimately depends on the tenacity and sincerity of the doer. Action is always better than inaction.

Action inspires hope, success and happiness whereas inaction invariably leads to fear, anxiety and depression. One good act leads to another and by using each day with enthusiasm and hard work, life becomes a saga of success, joy and acclaim. It sets an example that motivates others to use their day down to the minutes, and make life happy and successful.

> ### Learning Points:
> ▸ You may delay, but time will not, and lost time is never found again.
> ▸ The secret of success lies in not only striking the iron while it is hot but also in striking it forcefully and repeatedly.
> ▸ By using each day with enthusiasm and hard work, life becomes a saga of success, joy and acclaim.

Chapter 25

Being with Nature

'Look deep into nature, and then you will understand everything better.'

—Albert Einstein, German theoretical physicist

In the present context of life, most of our waking hours are spent looking at some screen, whether it's a mobile phone, laptop, desktop, tablet or television. Our eyes are never off a screen. It has made life quite mechanical, dull and mundane. It is, indeed, essential to find time and be outdoors with nature. It may be a park, a garden, boating in a lake or river, visiting beaches or planning a visit to some forest area or a national park. Spending time with nature enriches our life, as it gives us an opportunity and a proper setting to be with ourselves and connect with our souls.

Nature Connects Us

Whenever we are in a park or garden, there is an unconscious desire to search for a proper place and sit-down. Once we sit down, our thoughts differ from our routine thinking. The first thought comes about the place itself, its design, flowers, and trees, and so on. But very soon we start thinking about ourselves, our own existence, joys and sorrows and various other aspects of life. If we remain there for quite some time, we are bound to contemplate issues we normally do not entertain. Nature makes us connect with ourselves, our inner being. Being with nature makes us peaceful and encourages contemplation.

Nature Makes Us Joyful

Mahatma Gandhi said, 'To forget how to dig the earth and to tend the soil is to forget ourselves.' A large part of stress, anxiety and joylessness in life today may be ascribed to the lack of our connect with nature. It is true that touching the soil, walking barefoot on green and dew-moist lawn in the morning, watching a sunrise and sunset, looking at a serene blue sky in the day and a starlit one in the night are divine experiences that elevate our mood and make us vibrant and joyful.

Henry David Thoreau, the great American naturalist and philosopher, said, 'I took a walk in the woods and came out taller than the trees.' He further adds, 'Live in each season as it passes; breathe the air, drink the drink, taste the fruit, and resign yourself to the influence of the earth.'

Be with Nature

Nature has varied forms of life, colour and fragrance, harsh and soft moods, drizzling as well as torrential rains, snow-capped mountains and deserts, and many more contrasting features; in all these aspects, there is something unique and marvellous that connects us to our roots, to ourselves and to our souls. To be happy in life, it's essential to unplug by making efforts to be with nature, if possible on a daily basis or at least once or twice a week.

Vincent van Gogh, the Dutch painter, once said, 'And then, I have nature and art and poetry, and if that is not enough, what is enough?'

Learning Points:

- Nature makes us connect with ourselves—our inner being.
- A large part of stress, anxiety and joylessness in life today may be ascribed to the lack of our connect with nature.
- Being with nature makes us peaceful and encourages contemplation.

Chapter 26

Create Your Destiny

'You are the creator of your own destiny.'

—Swami Vivekananda, Indian Hindu monk and philosopher

The Buddha said that the past is behind us, the future has not yet arrived and only the present moment is available to live and cherish. We should learn to live and enjoy every moment of our life. It's useless to wait for something to happen tomorrow to make us happy. Our lives are made up of moments, minutes, hours and days. We do not have an infinite time span. Mother Teresa, catholic nun and Nobel laureate, said, 'Be happy in the moment, that's enough. Each moment is all we need, not more.'

Make Each Moment Count

We know that nothing in life occurs by chance or happens by accident. We must create our own destiny by utilizing opportunities and using each moment of our life wisely and creatively. The importance of every moment may not be distinct, yet each moment in life matters and is crucial in making our life happy and significant.

Ralph Waldo Emerson wrote, 'Write it on your heart that every day is the best day in the year.' To live a life of joy, we should try to fully use each moment of the day and learn to make it perfect. We should do something different that has beauty and purpose, as each day is an important unit of the mosaic of life.

Present Is the Foundation of the Future

The past is important, as it gives us an opportunity to ponder on the journey and learn our lessons. We may decide not to repeat the mistakes that we committed in the past and improve upon our good deeds and positive aspects of life. It is true that many things get lost or passed over with the passage of time. Our relationships with our parents or growing children cannot be re-lived once our parents are gone or our children have grown up and made their own lives.

Present moments are successors to the past and any structure for the present is raised on the foundation of the past. This is equally true about our vision, dreams and plans. Therefore, the importance of living the present moment with full focus, drive and energy is extremely crucial for a beautiful and meaningful edifice of life. The way we live, celebrate and conduct ourselves each moment on a daily basis prepares the ground and acts as a foundation for our future life.

Nothing Is More Precious than Time

Stephen R. Covey, American educator and author of *The 7 Habits of Highly Effective People*, says, 'The key is not in "spending" time, but in "investing" it.' Covey means that one should invest each moment of life in creating something worthwhile, having value and significance. We take time for granted and think that time is free, but nothing is more precious than time. We can use it wisely and creatively but can never own it or keep it.

Once a moment is lost, it's lost forever. We all want to live a life of health, joy and beauty. Therefore, we should value time and never waste it. Life is made up of minutes, and each minute has only 60 seconds. The point has been highlighted time and again by eminent people in history.

American cartoonist Bil Keane rightly said, 'Yesterday is the past, tomorrow's the future, but today is a gift. That's why it's called present.' Similarly, Charles Darwin wrote, 'A man who dares to waste one hour of time has not discovered the value of life.'

Learning Points:

- We should learn to live and enjoy every moment of our life.
- Nothing in life occurs by chance or happens by accident.
- We must create our own destiny by using each moment of our life wisely and creatively.

Chapter 27

Eating Is an Art

'Thou shouldst eat to live; not live to eat.'

—Socrates, Greek philosopher

For a joyful life, a balanced lifestyle—in food, conduct, recreation, sleep and wakefulness—is of the highest importance. Food is very crucial for our health; it needs special attention and should not be neglected. One should eat and drink with one's full focus and whole heart.

Eating Intelligently Is an Art

Many of us eat our breakfast in a hurry. At lunch, the rush of the day does not allow us to plan what we eat, and at dinner also, we are never at peace. Logically, dinner should be taken quietly but often it is taken seated as a group while talking and, quite often, using mobile phones in between. Thus, we are always in a hurry while eating.

Focus on the Act of Eating

For health and happiness, one should eat one's meals with focus on the act of eating. While eating food, our mind should be quiet and haste should be avoided. Food taken with calmness and a sense of gratitude affects our health and thoughts in a positive way.

We are aware that the food we eat passes through many stages; further, many people are involved in our food before it reaches our table. Consuming food in a hurry is 'in a way', not recognizing the efforts and contribution of people involved in the process. It also amounts to not being grateful to the bounty of nature, which nourishes the grain, fruits and other ingredients of the food. Ignoring the love and affection of the people involved in preparing and serving us is also a significant act of ingratitude.

Moderation in Life

Deepak Chopra, author of the *The New York Times* bestseller, *The Seven Spiritual Laws of Success*, says, 'The way you think, the way you behave, the way you eat, can influence your life by 30 to 50 years.' While eating, we should keep in mind that moderation in the quantity of food we eat is the key for a healthy body and sound mind. Bhagavad Gita emphasizes the importance of moderation in all aspects of our activities for joyful living. Lord Krishna in the Gita exhorts Arjuna to exercise moderation in every aspect of life:

> *Yuktaharaviharasya yuktachestasyakarmasu*
> *Yuktasvapnavabodhasya yogo bhavati duhkhaha*

[For a person who is moderate in food, in actions and conduct, in sleep and waking, he acquires a discipline (yoga) which destroys all his sorrows.]

—Bhagavad Gita 6.17

According to the Gita, it is essential for a person to be temperate and appropriate in every conduct to alleviate pain and suffering from their life.

Be Grateful While Eating

Food should not be eaten simply to satisfy our hunger; rather it's an occasion to be peaceful, meditative and grateful for the gifts of life. While consuming food, we should be grateful to the people involved in its preparation at various stages and above all to the bounties of nature. The food we eat gives us energy to conduct our life in a healthy and sound manner and affects our thoughts and conduct.

Learning Points:

- Food eaten with calmness and a sense of gratitude affects our health and thoughts in a positive way.
- Moderation in quantity is essential for a healthy body and sound mind.
- For a joyful life, a balanced lifestyle is of the highest importance.

Chapter 28

Speaking Well Is an Art

'Speak sweetly and positively, for your words have the power to inspire and uplift.'

—Unknown

Speech is a great gift of God to human beings and should be used with a lot of discretion. We exchange our thoughts and emotions through our speech. Success or failure of a human being largely depends on the contents and manner of their speech. Truth, brevity, sweetness and warmth are crucial elements of a good speech. Sweet speech makes life sweet and comfortable. People well versed in speaking sweetly are welcome everywhere and earn goodwill and friends wherever they go.

Open New Avenues and Opportunities

Sweet speech multiplies the number of friends and opens doors, whereas harsh words create anger, enmity and unhappiness. It is said that the world is shaped by two things—stories told and the memories left behind. A leader endowed with sweet and warm speech has many well-wishers and followers as compared to one who lacks this gift.

Speak Sweetly to Others

There is a famous anecdote in the epic Mahabharata where the harsh and stinging words of the Pandava queen Draupadi enraged Duryodhan to the extent that he never forgot the humiliation. It initiated an unwelcome sequence of events that ultimately led to the greatest war of all times, resulting in tremendous loss of human life and destruction of the kingdom. Therefore, one should speak sweet words, as it agrees with all concerned and spreads joy and harmony around. A speech with harsh and unpleasant content not only adversely affects the listeners but also vitiates the environment, causing much strife and suffering that was avoidable.

The wisdom of the great saint and poet Kabir is worth emulating:

Aisi bani boliye, man ka aapaa khoy,
Aapan ko shital kare, auran ko sukh hoy.

[Speak such words, devoid of ego,
that keeps you cool, make others happy too.]

Words are precious and have an effect on listeners. Words make or mar moods, relationships and situations. They can sort out an intricate situation or can make it more complicated.

Speak Truthfully

To live a happy and meaningful life, discipline and discretion in speech is of paramount importance. In the Gita, Krishna exhorts Arjuna to speak words which are truthful, agreeable and beneficial:

Anudvegkaram vakyam satyam priyahitam cha yat,
Svadhyayabhyasanam chaiv vanmayam tapa uchyate.

[Speaking of words devoid of offence, being truthful, pleasant and beneficial; and the study of scriptures are said to be the penance of speech.]

—Bhagavad Gita 17.15

Speaking sweet and agreeable words has been called penance of speech in the Gita. The speech of a human being is a mirror of their views, beliefs and thoughts. It needs great practice and discipline to be cautious and balanced in speech. Most people are found wanting in this respect, and whenever they speak their feelings, their anger and aversion are conveyed to the listeners. Therefore, one should be careful while speaking and use only nice and sweet words fit for the occasion which do not cause hurt, agony or unpleasantness.

Speaking Well Is an Art

It is true that all of us speak sweet and agreeable words with our near and dear ones or the people we expect some favour from, but the real challenge lies in always speaking sweet and agreeable words with others. There we need discretion and proper balance in the tone, content and gesture of speaking.

In developing the art of good speech, the following wisdom of the ancient scripture is quite relevant:

Satyam bruyat priyam bruyannabruyat satyamapriyam
Priyam cha nanritam bruyadesa dharmah sanatanah

[One should speak the truth, and sweet; one should not speak a truth that is disagreeable; and also should not speak the agreeable that is not true—it is precept of the eternal law.]

—Manu Smriti 4.138

Agreeable speech appropriate to the occasion is very crucial for people in positions of authority and leadership, as their words carry tremendous influence and have far-reaching consequences. Dr Mardy Grothe, famous American psychologist and management consultant, has said, 'Words have incredible power. They can make people's hearts soar, or they can make people's hearts sore.'

While speaking, one should be careful about their choice of words, tone and content, as the message conveyed depends equally on what is said, and how it is said.

There is another school of thought which believes, 'Be who you are and say what you feel, because in the end those who matter don't mind, and those who mind don't matter.'

The irony of life is that even those who know you and matter do mind if the spoken words are not sweet and agreeable. Ultimately, we should understand that speaking is really an art and decisively affects one's success and quality of life. It is also true that we reap the seeds we sow. The fragrance of our words reaches far and wide and builds up our fame and reputation accordingly. Therefore, we should learn to speak sweet words in all situations and circumstances.

Learning Points:

▸ Speech is a great gift to human beings and should be used with a lot of discretion.
▸ Sweet speech multiplies the number of friends and opens doors, whereas harsh words create anger, enmity and unhappiness.
▸ One should be careful about the choice of words, tone and content, as the message conveyed depends equally on what is said and how it is said.

Chapter 29

Choose to Be Content

'The greatest wealth is to live content with little.'

—Plato, Greek philosopher

In simple words, contentment is a feeling of happy satisfaction. It is a state of being satisfied with what one has or whatever happens in life. It is the emotional state of being completely happy with life. It is said that contentment makes a poor man feel rich, and its absence makes even a super-rich person feel utterly poor. We are aware of the famous saying 'The grass is always greener on the other side.' We always belittle what we have and think what others have is better.

Being Content Depends on Challenges

The contentment one achieves from completing a task depends on the challenges and difficulties encountered in finishing it. If a task is easy, one may not derive great satisfaction on its completion. But if it is difficult, uncertain and has competition, its completion would provide a great sense of contentment. Therefore, to be happy, one should always be willing to take up tasks and assignments that involve challenges and require massive effort and application of resources.

Serving Brings Contentment

The scope of tasks and activities one is involved in also determines the degree of contentment. Routine activities do not give any satisfaction and make life dull and mundane. But the tasks that affect large number of people and are performed with a sense of service provide great contentment to the doers. Similarly, activities performed to benefit people without any selfish motive are also great sources of contentment.

Never Be Perturbed

Mark Twain wrote, 'Good friends, good books, and a sleepy conscience: this is the ideal life.' It is true that good friends and good books lead to positive thoughts and make life happy and content. Likewise, taking a balanced view of life's happenings, and not being unduly perturbed with adversities and people's reactions, is another powerful tool to be content and happy in life.

No End to Wishes

Socrates wrote, 'Contentment is natural wealth, luxury is artificial poverty.'

Our happiness is an inner phenomenon and so is contentment. It depends on our views on life. A man is as happy and content as he chooses to be. Plato said that the greatest wealth is to live content with little. There is no end to wishes and desires. If we are content with what we have, and feel happy with our situation, we will find that lack of material objects does not affect our peace and happiness.

Contentment is an inner sense of satisfaction, a way of life, a strong belief in a bigger scheme of things and an attitude that whatever happens in life is for the good. It entirely depends on our own disposition towards life. It is independent of external factors and circumstances.

Learning Points:

- Contentment is a state of being happy and satisfied with what one has or whatever happens in life.
- Contentment makes a poor man feel rich, and its absence makes even the super-rich feel utterly poor.
- It entirely depends on our own attitude and is independent of external factors and circumstances.

Chapter 30

Joyful Existence for All

'Sometimes your joy is the source of your smile, but sometimes your smile can be the source of your joy.'

—Thich Nhat Hanh, Buddhist monk

A joyful existence should not be difficult for anybody. But ego and distorted notions of reality are major hurdles in the path of happiness. We see people and events with a narrow vision and fail to grasp a holistic view of things and situations. Likewise, our ego and the habit of being self-centred prohibit us from appreciating the virtues and goodness of other people.

Awareness and Understanding

The lack of appreciation of reality and a self-centred attitude colour our vision, and affect our thoughts and conduct. Instead of viewing things as they are, we create our own reality based on our preferences and prejudices. It creates barriers between us and other people and hinders free communication and appreciation of things. To be joyful in life, it is essential to understand people and circumstances in the proper perspective and see things as they really are. Right understanding and awareness can lead to a peaceful and happy existence.

Life Is More than Just Pleasure

Stress and anxiety arise due to our misplaced notions, expectations and desires from life. We must understand that both pleasure and pain are inevitable parts of life. The objects of pleasure—food, fragrance, music, beauty and touch—affect us at the sensorial level. These feelings are fleeting and temporary. They last while we are experiencing them. These pleasures lose their meaning if we are emotionally disturbed or if our mind is agitated. Therefore, we should have a balanced attitude towards life and should not stake all for these fleeting sensations. Life is much more than this.

Emotional Well-Being

Our genuine happiness depends on our mental state as sensorial pleasures do not last long. Over a period, the objects of pleasure lose their significance. Happiness is related with a feeling of mental fulfilment and satisfaction at a conscious level. Sensorial pleasures can be a contributing factor but never a cause for joyful existence on a durable basis. What really matters in life is peace, calmness and emotional balance. Other contributing causes for emotional well-being are kindness, compassion, contentment, love and forgiveness.

No Man Is an Island

Happiness does not depend only on the individual, as the family, community and society in which the individual lives also affect one's quality of life. Howsoever powerful and resourceful a person may be, they cannot survive alone. To be happy, a positive and agreeable community behaviour and favourable environment is needed. There lies the importance of emotional bond with the family and society.

At an emotional level, human beings are wired to protect themselves and their near and dear ones from external forces and untoward incidents. Love, affection and a sense of belonging are part of our instinct that helps us to survive and enhance our happiness in life. Extending affection not only to human beings and animals but to all life forms and the environment is known as compassion.

A Happy Community

Joyful existence in the community can be ensured only when our mental horizon is expanded, and the sense of separation and differentiation is reduced to a minimum. The old precept of *Vasudhaiva Kutumbakam*, or 'the world is one family' is a profound thought to ensure joyful existence for all. If acted upon sincerely by all concerned, it can usher in a society where everyone thinks and acts to make everyone happy and joyful. In the present context of critical climate issues, this concept has become extremely relevant and can prove a great tool not only in saving the Earth but in making the world a much better and joyful place. It has the potential to make the world a genuinely happy family.

Humanity Must Join Hands

Vasudhaiva Kutumbakam is part of a famous Sanskrit shloka appearing in the Panchatantra and Hitopadesh. It underlines the importance of treating the whole world as a family. While this precept has wide acceptance at thought level, the conduct of people has not been in accordance with this.

In light of the world turning into a global village due to ever-expanding means of communication and transportation, the time to make it a central theme of thought and action by all countries in the world has already arrived. In view of the challenges of climate change and global warming causing irreversible environmental degradation, humanity must join hands and work as a family to save the planet, and thus save humanity from inevitable extinction.

Co-operation Is the Way to Go

The problems of distrust, conflict and violence due to racial discrimination, narrowing visions of nationality and skewed distribution of wealth, resulting in poverty and suffering in almost all parts of the world, have reached dangerous proportions such that a new norm of thought and conduct has become inevitable. It calls for a new approach to save the planet and ensure joyful existence for all. There is a crying need to pause, think and co-operate with one another not only at the level of family and community but also at the level of the nations for a safe, peaceful and joyful existence for all.

Learning Points:

- Howsoever powerful and resourceful a person may be, they cannot survive alone.
- Happiness does not depend only on an individual, as the family, community and society decisively affect one's quality of life.
- There is a crying need to pause, think and co-operate not only at the level of family and society but also at the level of the nations for a safe and joyful existence for all.

PART 4

THE CONQUEST OF HAPPINESS

Chapter 31

Solitude Enriches Life

'Solitude is not the absence of company, but the moment when our soul is free to speak to us and help us decide what to do with our life.'

—Paulo Coelho, Brazilian novelist and lyricist

Being alone is often considered an undesirable and uncomfortable situation. But it is true that being alone gives one time and space to be in tune with one's inner being. Henry David Thoreau wrote, 'I love to be alone. I never found the companion that was so companionable as solitude.'

It is true that one is born alone, lives alone and leaves the world alone. It is the love and affection of family and friends which creates an illusion of not being alone, and thus we develop a feeling of comfort living in a family and in groups. In such a context, being alone seems to be an undesirable situation leading to anxiety and suffering. But the truth is that being alone is a highly desirable situation that enables us to think deeply, connect with our inner self and feel comfortable in our own skin.

Being Alone Can Be a Boon

Being alone does not mean being lonely and unhappy. If we want to be genuinely happy, we should develop a habit of being in solitude for some time on a regular basis and enrich our lives. Pablo Picasso said, 'Without great solitude, no serious work is possible.' It is true that we need to be alone to ponder over complex situations arising in life and think of the pros and cons of steps to be taken. Decisions taken in a hurry always spoil the game and invite adverse consequences. Therefore, it is essential to sit alone and thoroughly examine all the aspects of a problem before taking a final call about important issues in life. And then, if needed, ensure some mid-course corrections. It is said that an unexamined life is no life.

The Importance of Solitude

In ancient times, seers and sages used to live in forest and mountains, devoting their time towards the study of scriptures, contemplation and teaching. They understood the importance of solitude. Living with nature and observing wildlife, studying amidst the chirping of birds and the sounds of rushing rivers used to be the great setting in which the Vedas, Upanishads and other scriptures were conceived and revealed.

In the modern context, it is often not possible nor desirable to live in a forest or on top of a mountain. However, being alone and disconnected from people for some time in a day or a week is highly desirable, as it may give a sense of peace and serenity. It may enable a person to have a new perspective towards life and thus rediscover themselves. Time spent in peace and solitude enriches one's experience and can give a new direction to life and its meaning.

The Fear of Loneliness

In normal life, we are so used to living in the company of people that being alone seems to be a great misery and torture. One feels undesired and unloved and many people suffer bouts of anxiety and depression. But for a meaningful and creative life, one should develop the habit of solitude by design and learn to enjoy it. To enjoy the benefits of solitude, one must overcome the fear of being alone and consider it a great opportunity and privilege.

Solitude Feeds Creativity

There are many benefits of spending time in solitude, as it brings clarity to the mind, improves creativity and enables a person to explore new possibilities in their life. In the rush of life, we have no time or occasion to ponder over the direction in which our life is moving. Being alone gives us an opportunity to slow down and reset our priorities. One becomes much more focussed, confident and better connected with one's inner self and to the world around.

Learning Points:

- It is true that being alone gives time and space to be in tune with our inner being.
- Being alone does not mean being lonely and unhappy.
- Being alone gives us an opportunity to slow down and reset our priorities.

Chapter 32

Listen to the Inner Voice

'Listening to the inner voice—trusting the inner voice—is one of the most important lessons of leadership.'

—Warren G. Bennis, American organizational consultant and author

An often-heard piece of wisdom is that one should listen to one's inner voice without caring what others think and speak. It is a common observation that there is a voice inside us that counsels us as to what is right and what is wrong. Many thinkers believe that no parent, friend or elder can really guide us on what is right or wrong for us. We need to be sensitive to the voice that resides inside us. In a Stanford University commencement speech in 2005, Steve Jobs said, 'Don't let the noise of others' opinions drown out your own inner voice.'

Be Attentive

It is true that there is infinite wisdom and immense creative force in our being and this can be a true guide in the journey of life. We should be attentive to this inner voice and give due importance to it. If we have faith and respect the voice, we can always access the great reservoir of wisdom lying buried in our own consciousness. Ralph Waldo Emerson said, 'Belief consists in accepting the affirmation of the soul; unbelief, in denying them.'

It May Be Quiet

Life is full of struggles and there is always a dilemma in choosing a right course of action. People are more than ready to advise others about the right course of action in any and every situation. When so much advice and wisdom is floating around, one should always prioritize the voice from within. It may be a quiet and gentle one, but is still worth listening to and acting upon. American novelist and poet Richelle E. Goodrich said, 'To mute all other voices but one's own, to live true to that voice—that is being bold.'

Divinity Resides Within

All scriptures proclaim that God resides within us, and if we have faith and are in constant communion with our inner self, it will always guide us to the right path. In the Bhagavad Gita, Krishna advises Arjuna:

Uddharedatmanatmanam natmanamavasdayet,
Atmaiva hyatmano bandhuratmaiva ripuratmanah.

[Let a man elevate himself by himself; let him not degrade himself, for the self alone is the friend of the self, and the self alone is the enemy of the self.]

—Bhagavad Gita 6.5

Heed Your Inner Voice

It is obvious that nobody can advise us as well as our own self. But due to the hassles of life and influence of extrinsic forces, we are not able to listen to our inner whispers. We are drowned in the noise of the world and get confused about our true welfare. Mahatma Gandhi says, 'Everyone who wills can hear the inner voice. It is within everyone.'

If we trust this inner voice, it will always give us valuable advice and lead us to the right path. As we become attuned to our inner voice, life becomes a saga of joy and happiness.

> **Learning Points:**
> - There is a voice inside us that counsels us about right and wrong.
> - It may be a quiet and gentle one but is still worth listening to and acting upon.
> - If we trust this inner voice, it will always give us valuable advice and lead us to the right path.

Chapter 33

The Gita Can Transform Life

'The Bhagavada Gita is the most important philosophical and spiritual classic ever written.'

—Aldous Huxley, British writer and philosopher

All of us want a life that is stress-free and joyful. We all wish for success, happiness and a fulfilling life. We do our best to achieve these goals with energy and enthusiasm. But everybody, irrespective of their age, is suffering from anxiety and depression in varying degrees. Nowadays, even the young are becoming victims of severe anxiety and depression. There is anxiety and stress in every relationship, as warm and enduring relationships are becoming rarer.

The Gita Can Transform

At such a juncture in society, the Gita appears to be one of the most relevant guides to transform one's thoughts and actions. The Gita holds wisdom that can guide people to a life of joy and meaning. It recognizes no taboos or limitations for living a joyful life. Its wisdom can elevate the life of a person in various respects. The Gita helps us in living an exalted life free of stress, anxiety and worries. The Gita informs us about various categories of human beings, the nature of the world and the ways to deal with it.

The Gita Teaches Happiness

The Gita teaches us how to be happy and content in life and how to cope with heat and cold, joy and suffering, and success and failure without being perturbed. It advises us about different kinds of actions and their consequences. It also offers wisdom to conduct ourselves with calm and equanimity. It describes very clearly that whatever is pleasing in the beginning will result in grief and suffering. Likewise, whatever appears hard and painful initially is sure to result in joy and happiness.

Shun the Whims of Desire

The Gita says that the choice of actions is in one's own hands, and with careful use of intellect and practice, life can become a journey of joy and bliss. One must be alert and conscious of the free play of passion and desire, and conduct one's life with due intellect and caution. The major obstacles in the path of a joyful life are the dictates of desire and passion, and a free run of the mind with its whims and fancies.

Therefore, we should cultivate divine habits and shun lust, anger and greed in order to live a happy and abundant life. When our attitude changes, our thoughts and actions also change. If we shift our focus from appropriating to giving, and from receiving to charity and sacrifice, we find that our life is totally transformed. Life becomes full of joy and peace with a new surge of creativity and enthusiasm. An entirely new chapter of life opens, and one experiences an elevated and joyful existence. Living with the spirit of service and sacrifice, we can transcend the mundane aspects, and lead a peaceful, joyful and sublime life.

Treat Everyone Well

One of the greatest lessons of the Gita is to rise above the limitations of differentiation and separateness, and treat everyone the way one likes himself to be treated. Lord Krishna emphasizes the importance of treating everyone equally.

> *Yo mam pashyati sarvatra sarvam cha mayi pashyati.*
> *Tasyaham na pranashyami sa cha me na pranashyati*
>
> [For those who see Me everywhere and see all things in me, I am never lost, nor are they ever lost to Me.]
>
> —Bhagavad Gita 6.30

By following even the basic tenets of the Gita, our life can be elevated to one of great success and blissful existence.

Learning Points:

- The Gita comprises wisdom that can guide people to lead a life of joy and meaning.
- The Gita helps us in living an exalted life free of stress, anxiety and worries.
- One of the greatest lessons of the Gita is to rise above the limitations of differentiation and treat everyone the way one wants to be treated.

Chapter 34

Pay No Attention

'Remain unmoved even when the eight winds blow.'

—Zen proverb

Words are magic, words are magnets and words are important. Buddhist wisdom also advises us to 'pay no attention'.

We come across situations in life when we are hurt by the words spoken by people. Sometimes, even the words spoken by our elders, even if they are said with the intent of helping us improvize, hurt us and appear to be unpleasant, harsh and cruel. This is due to our sensitivity and habit of paying attention to the opinion of others. We judge our worth by what others think or say about us. This is the root of all our hurt, unhappiness and sufferings.

Habit of Detachment

To be at peace with ourselves and the world, it is necessary to develop a habit of measured detachment, and not be swayed by others' thinking about us. If we are keen to live a life of joy and hope, we should try to remain unaffected by external influences and circumstances.

'The eight winds' described by Nichiren Daishonin in the Zen proverb quoted above are eight kinds of influences. Out of these, four are favourable influences and the other four adverse. Nichiren encouraged his disciples not to succumb to influences that obstruct one's joy and peace. The four positive influences that people tend to seek are prosperity, honour, praise and pleasure; the adverse four that people are keen to shun and avoid are decline, disgrace, censure and suffering.

Shun Three Evils

The pursuit of happiness has been a constant endeavour of human beings since ages. We all want to be happy and joyful. We are ever keen to avoid the things that make us sad and unhappy. Sages and scholars have seriously pondered over the issue of happiness as well as the things that need to be shunned for a joyful life. In the Bhagavad Gita, Krishna cautions Arjuna to shun lust, anger and greed for a life of joy and substance:

Trividham narakasyedam dvaaram naashanamaatmanah.
Kaamah krodhastathaa lobhastasmaadetattrayam tyajet.

[Lust, anger and greed, these are three which degrade the soul and lead one to the doors of hell. Therefore, one must shun these three evils.]

—Bhagavad Gita 16.21

The above shloka says that lust, anger and greed destroy a person's moral fabric and lead to their downfall. These evils cause a person to deviate from the right path and that they are doorways to hell. Therefore, to lead a life of joy and happiness, one should shun these evils.

Adopting an Attitude of Detachment

The pertinent point is how to shun and avoid these evils, and remain untouched by lust, anger and greed. Saints, sages and scriptures in all societies have recommended various ways to shun these vices to lead a life of joy, peace and harmony. The simplest way is to develop an attitude of indifference towards the charms of the world, and not get trapped in the web of dualities. One should take praise and criticism, as well as joy and pain in one's stride. The cardinal principle is not to be charmed by favourable influences and deterred by adverse events and situations.

The best way to do so is to do one's duty and discharge one's responsibilities with an attitude of detachment towards material things, happenings and the bond of relationships. One should see the world from a measured distance and try to lead a life without being unduly affected by the bonds of blood and gold.

Learning Points:

- Words are magic, words are magnets and words are important.
- For a life of joy and hope, we should try to remain unaffected by external influences and circumstances.
- Try to lead a life without being unduly affected by the bonds of blood and gold.

Chapter 35

The Right Moment

'Do not wait for the right moment; create it'.

—George Bernard Shaw, playwright, critic, polemicist and political activist

Many people believe that life is an enigma, a mystery, and a puzzle to solve. We must be alert and attentive every moment of our life, as even slight carelessness may lead to a wrong decision and missed opportunities. Some believe that everything happens at its right moment and for a cause. It happens neither too soon nor too late. Human beings have limits to which they can change the course of their life.

The Right Moment

Paulo Coelho said, 'The two hardest tests on the spiritual road are the patience to wait for the right moment, and the courage not to be disappointed with what we encounter.' Life has always been a matter of waiting for the right moment to take the call and act. A popular proverb says one should strike the iron while it is hot. Another says that one should go on striking the iron until it becomes hot. A person must choose the moment when he should really strike the iron. Life's success and failure depend on this choice and this choice alone.

Wait for It

The best policy for success in life lies in acting at the right moment. One should not try to force things but just watch the flow of events and the drift of happenings, and take a call at the right moment. Due to our preoccupation with mundane affairs of life, it is difficult to judge the right moment. Quite often, it leads to hasty decisions resulting in undesirable consequences and disappointments. Life is a game of choosing that right moment.

When a Door Closes

Every day presents a new problem and a new opportunity before us. It depends on our readiness to tackle it and move forward in a desired direction. Prima facie, it appears to be naive to wait for the right moment and not take the plunge. There are numerous instances of success where taking a call on the spur of the moment has resulted in historic achievements. But the common wisdom is always to take a call with due thinking and discretion. It is also true that a moment becomes right due to the application of grit, courage and initiative.

The wisdom lies in facing the obstacles and staying the course. However, it is always better to assess the situation and act when the circumstances appear favourable and when one is ready. When a door closes in front of us, we should not get perturbed, for not every door is meant for us. The right door shall open at the right time, provided we are ready for it.

Be Ready and Alert

For success and happiness in life, acting at the right time is wisdom. But it is also true that life is not an endless affair. Our life is limited with the constraints of time and space. The trend today is to move fast and aggressively and be the first to reach the right place and avail the opportunity. In this context, waiting for the right time may amount to not reaching the place at all.

There is competition in every field of life, and people are rushing to be the first to avail the chances life offers. In such situations, one has the option to rush or wait with patience for the right moment. The secret lies in moving ahead towards the destination with measured steps and keep looking forward. Life is nothing but a succession of moments, and to live each moment to its full possibility is to succeed and live well.

If we are ready and alert, we shall know the moment that's right for us.

Learning Points:

- Our life is limited within the constraints of time and space.
- We must be alert and attentive every moment of our life.
- Life is a matter of waiting for the right moment to take a call and act.

Chapter 36

A Spiritual Life

'Spirituality is the recognition of our true nature, our divine essence.'

—Deepak Chopra, Indian–American author

A spiritual life is nothing but following spiritual values in life, listening to your inner voice and walking your talk. A spiritual life does not mean visiting temples, keeping a fast, worshipping gods and practising religious rituals. Careful contemplation may reveal that offering water and milk, flower and fragrance, reciting mantras or prayers and doing charity cannot fulfil our wishes or grant us what we desire in this life or beyond.

Divinity in Conscience

The great scholar of Vedic philosophy Acharya Shriram Sharma said, 'The universal truth is that the power of divinity is not there in the idol of a deity; it is not awakened by any rituals. Divinity dwells in the depths of your conscience, purity of your mind and heart.'

Ritual practices may lead to positive results only if

performed with great devotion, pure intellect and complete faith in the divine power. To reach this stage requires rigorous training of the body and mind, inculcating great human virtues, and living a virtuous and austere life.

A Life of Virtues

Spirituality is being sensitive to your inner voice and not getting lost in material aspects of life. A spiritual life pertains to refinement of thoughts, speech and actions. It is living a life of virtues, truthfulness and compassion. It is living in peace and harmony with fellow human beings and nature. A life that makes one feel joyful and is devoted to making others happy can be called a true spiritual life.

Being in Peace and Harmony

The main attributes of a spiritual life are being in peace, harmony and a joyful state. The acts of a spiritual person are always guided by the belief that God is present in every being. The other qualities of a spiritual person are empathy, optimism, compassion and love for all beings. Krishna highlights the quality of such a person in the Gita:

Sarvabhuteshu yenaikam bhavamavyayameekshate
Avibhaktam vibhakteshu tatgyanam viddhi sattvikam.

[The knowledge by which a person sees one undivided imperishable reality within all diverse living beings is of sattvik kind.]

—Bhagavad Gita 18.20

This verse conveys the profound unity of all living beings. When we are spiritual, we become one with the whole stream of life and see no differentiation. We develop a sense of brotherhood, empathy and compassion for all. This is the essence of a spiritual life.

A Spiritual Life

The Buddha said, 'What you think, you become. What you feel, you attract. What you imagine, you create.'

Living a spiritual life involves thinking good of all, feeling empathy for all, and living an egoless, virtuous and simple life. Swami Vivekananda says that to lead a spiritual life you must grow from inside out as none can teach or make you spiritual. There is no other teacher but your own conscience.

A joyful life is nothing but living one's life with love, gratitude and compassion. Such a life can be called a spiritual life.

Learning Points:

- A spiritual life does not mean visiting temples, keeping fasts, worshipping gods and practising religious rituals.
- A spiritual life is nothing but following spiritual values, listening to your inner voice and walking your talk.
- Spirituality dwells in the depths of one's conscience, in the purity of one's mind and heart.

Chapter 37

Meditation Transforms

'Meditation is not a means to an end. It is both the means and the end.'

—Jiddu Krishnamurti, Indian philosopher, speaker and writer

The process of thinking is closely related with the state of mind. The human mind is of extremely wavering nature and it is very difficult to focus on any object or thought for long. One is not able to think properly if the mind is agitated. But if the mind is at peace, one can easily engage in profound thoughts and concentrate on any subject for long.

Sitting Peacefully Has Become Rare

One can devote one's attention to a particular issue at will but deep contemplation is only possible when one is at peace with oneself. We are aware of the importance of sitting quietly and pondering issues important to us.

But in today's rushed life, it is rare to have time and intent to sit peacefully and have a dialogue with oneself. We are always in a hurry and almost all our decisions are taken in haste and on an ad-hoc basis. This is one of the major reasons for anxiety, depression and other psychosomatic disorders. A restless mind is the main hurdle for a healthy, happy and joyful life.

Meditation Is Quietening the Mind

For success and happiness in life, we should make decisions after proper thinking and considering all pros and cons with a peaceful mind. Meditation is one of the most important tools available to us for developing a calm and quiet disposition.

Meditation is nothing but quietening the mind and witnessing its agitation in a detached manner. Patanjali said, 'Undisturbed calmness of mind is attained by cultivating friendliness towards the happy, compassion for the unhappy, delight in the virtuous, and indifference toward the wicked.' Meditation is entering the inner recesses of our mind and experiencing the undisturbed calmness of our being.

The Soul Speaks to a Quiet Mind

It is said that if we quieten our mind, the soul will speak to us. For a joyful life, it is important to be calm and quiet. Meditation is the best tool to quieten the mind. When we are in meditation, agitation disappears and we can feel immense peace and serenity in our being. If we meditate deeply on a regular basis, very soon we start acting from a centre of peace and calmness; our mind becomes quiet and still. Such a mind has been equated in the Gita with the flame of a candle in a windless place:

*Yathaa deepo nivaatastho nengate sopamaa smritaa
Yogino yatachittasya yunjato yogamaatmanah*

[As the flame of a lamp does not flicker in a windless place, such is the state of mind of a yogi practising meditation.]

—Bhagavad Gita 6.19

A Powerful Technique

Meditation is a powerful technique for transforming our mind, our life and our self. It is observing our thoughts, witnessing our mind's agitation, and transcending its wavering to reach our deep and calm consciousness. The objective of meditation is not to stop or control thoughts, as that is against the very nature of the mind. It is to regulate the mind's wavering and not to permit it to dictate our thoughts and deeds.

Transforming Life

Meditation opens new vistas of thinking, new possibilities and transforms a person's life. It has been found to improve physical, intellectual and psychological health of people. Meditation can instil a unique calmness and blissful silence in our frenetic routine of life. It ensures better cognitive functioning and enhances our creativity. Regular meditation ensures better relationships, greater professional success and a healthy and joyful life. It leads to self-actualization and has been found to result in a calm, quiet and happy state of mind.

Learning Points:

- Meditation is one of the most important tools available to develop a calm and quiet disposition.
- Meditation is nothing but quietening the mind and witnessing its agitation in a detached manner.
- Meditation opens new vistas of thinking, new possibilities and transforms a person's life.

Chapter 38

Excessive Indulgence

'Everything in excess is opposed to nature.'

—Hippocrates, Greek physician, Father of Medicine

A well-balanced life is said to be a joyful life. A balanced life is characterized by a sense of peace and harmony. A person of balanced mindset is in full control of their life. Such a person is not in haste and never acts on an ad-hoc basis. There is no excess and extremism in the thoughts and actions of such a person. We all know that excess of anything is bad and should be avoided.

Atidanaddhatah Karnastv atilobhat Suyodhanah
Atikamaddashagrivahstv ati sarvatra varjayet

[Due to excessive charity, Karna was killed, due to excessive greed, Suyodhan (Duryodhan); due to excessive lust, Ravana was killed—excess of everything is bad.]

—Maha-Subhashita-Samgraha, 562

The ancient aphorism *'ati sarvatra varjayet'* mentioned in the above shloka of Maha-Subhashita-Samgrah says that excessive indulgence should be shunned. In fact, too much of anything is bad and should be given up. But, in life, people become oblivious of this wisdom and exceed the limits of moderation, ultimately facing its adverse consequences. This is true in every aspect of human life. For a joyful living, one should never throw balance and moderation to the winds.

Excess Is Bad

The verse from where the above aphorism is taken gives clear examples from Indian mythology to state its significance. The verse that concludes in 'ati sarvatra varjayet' refers to the epics to drive home this wisdom. It gives the example of King Bali who had to face the wrath of God because of his ego born of excessive charity practised by him. The virtue of charity is highly exalted in society but excess virtues can lead to disastrous results, as it invariably heightens the ego of the doer.

Other examples in this context are those of Ravana and Duryodhana, who met their doom due to excessive pride and greed. They lost the sense of balance in their thoughts and deeds and invited their own destruction. There are numerous such examples across ages and societies to prove that excess of everything is bad and disastrous.

Balance and Moderation

In the above examples, despite being brave and ruling great kingdoms, the two rulers Ravana and Duryodhana lacked balance and excessively indulged their ego, lust and pride, all of which resulted in defeat, disgrace and disrepute for both.

Therefore, for a meaningful and joyful life balance and moderation are the qualities one should never lose sight of.

Excessive Greed and Anger

Despite being counselled by Vidur, Bhishma, Dronacharya and even Lord Krishna, wisdom did not dawn upon Duryodhana in the Mahabharata. Due to his excessive ego and greed, aided by extreme anger and jealousy towards the Pandavas, he could not act with justice and fair play regarding the rights of his cousins, the Pandavas. With Dronacharya as his guru, Bhishma as his guardian adviser and the wise counsel of Vidur, Duryodhana still could not understand the realities on the ground. He insisted on depriving the Pandavas of their rightful share in the kingdom and violated all norms of justice and fair play. His conduct was solely responsible for the great war of the Mahabharata, which resulted in destruction, annihilation and the end of an era.

The Cause of Ravana's Doom

The story of Ravana is similar; his excessive pride and lust did not allow him to appreciate the reality and brought about his own doom. His lust and ego led him to abduct Sita and carry her to Lanka across the sea. Even after his capital was burnt, wisdom did not dawn upon him, and Ravana refused to listen to the counsel of his ministers, his queen and other well-wishers of the family. He never agreed to listen to the voice of reason and return Sita. Consequently, a decisive war had to be fought with Lord Rama that led to the destruction of his clan and kingdom.

It Spoils Peace and Happiness

The main reason that people indulge in excess is their short-sighted vision, excessive greed and too much pride, all of which make them oblivious to the right wisdom. Such people lack balance and moderation in their thoughts and conduct. They are neither able to ponder the right course of action with a calm and balanced mind nor are they ready to follow the advice given to them by their family, friends and well-wishers.

Their excessive ego, pride and greed overshadows other good qualities and vitiates their thoughts and decision-making in every aspect of life. This excess harms people in many ways and makes them feel insecure and ill at ease; it also invariably affects the thoughts and conduct of their children and other dependents. It spoils their peace and happiness and creates complications of various kinds, and exacts a very heavy price from them.

It is true that excessive ego and lack of balance not only makes a person unduly proud and egotistical but also sets a bad precedent and allows unworthy models of conduct in society. It leads to avoidable conflict and violence that affect peace and harmony and vitiates the general fabric of social order.

Therefore, the main mantra for a joyful living is to practise balance and moderation in one's thoughts, speech and actions and avoid excess in all aspects of life.

> **Learning Points:**
> - Excessive indulgence in anything is bad and should be shunned.
> - A person of balanced disposition is never in haste and does not act on an ad-hoc basis.
> - The main mantra for a joyful living is to practise balance and moderation in thought, speech and action.

Chapter 39

Be Happy

'Think of all the beauty still left around you and be happy.'

—Anne Frank, Jewish diarist and Holocaust victim

As a tradition in Indian society, when anybody greets an elderly person belonging to the extended family or community, he or she responds with the words words: Be happy. This means they are expressing wishes not only for physical health but also overall happiness and well-being. This traditional blessing indicates the genuine feelings of the elders to see the person healthy, happy and prosperous.

Sleeping Well

Similar blessings are common in all cultures and societies. In Botswana, in southern Africa, when people meet, the common solicitation is 'Have you slept well?' We all know of the importance of sound sleep for physical and mental health. Good sleep improves our concentration and productivity, and it enhances vitality and immunity. It has a positive effect on our emotional health and social interaction. This kind of solicitation in any society depicts its ethos and creates empathy, harmony and a strong sense of brotherhood.

Gross National Happiness

The concept of happiness has always been of paramount importance in all societies in the world. However, in the present context of stress, anxiety and depression due to the fast pace of life and declining family and social support, it has attracted attention of not only families and societies but also of governments and international organizations. In the recent past, Bhutan, a small country ensconced in the Himalayas, introduced the concept of Gross National Happiness as a policy tool of the government of Bhutan. Bhutan has designed indices that are used to measure the collective happiness and well-being of its people.

A Better Indicator

King Jigme Singye Wangchuck of Bhutan was the first to coin the phrase 'Gross National Happiness' in 1972 when he declared Gross National Happiness to be more important than Gross Domestic Product. The concept emphasizes that the government should ensure sustainable development with a holistic approach where equal importance is given to non-economic aspects of well-being while devising policies and programmes for growth and development of the nation.

This concept has found an echo across the world, as it is a better yardstick to measure the economic, social and cultural well-being of people. Many countries in the world have now taken steps to create separate ministries and organizations to measure, monitor and advise the government on enhancing the Gross National Happiness of their people.

The Present View of Life

The present view of life, which emphasizes the acquisition of wealth and means of comfort as the main objective of the human endeavour, has not only resulted in creating a privileged class in all societies at the cost of a large section of people but has also damaged the planet and caused serious problems of global warming and climate change. This has also made human beings behave like robots devoid of long-cherished human values of family, brotherhood, harmony, empathy, compassion and concern for people around.

Let Us Make 'Be Happy' Universal

The quest for wealth and comfort for oneself and one's family at any cost has become the main objective of the human endeavour today. It has quite adversely affected the quality of human life across all societies in the world. It has not only divided families and communities but also societies, countries and the world into categories, such as developed and underdeveloped, rich and poor, and majority and minority. Such divisions have caused hatred, animosity, inequality and all-pervading poverty in the world.

The concept of wishing people to 'be happy' needs to be re-established and acted upon in a genuine sense across the family, community, society and nation. It will create empathy and harmony in society and spread the message of happiness and well-being for the benefit of all.

It has the potential to make every human being healthy and rich, and ensure the wellness and well-being of people irrespective of caste, creed, race, religion and colour. Sincere efforts by all can usher in an era of universal joy and happiness and save our planet from the devastating effects of climate change and environmental degradation.

Learning Points:

▸ The traditional blessing of 'Be Happy' indicates the genuine feeling of elders for health, happiness and prosperity.
▸ Bhutan has introduced the concept of Gross National Happiness as a major policy tool of the government of Bhutan.
▸ The concept of 'Be happy' needs to be re-established and acted upon in a genuine sense across the family, community, society and nation.

Chapter 40

Lifetime Happiness

'Happiness is not something ready-made. It comes from your own actions.'

—His Holiness, the fourteenth Dalai Lama

Pablo Picasso said, 'The meaning of life is to find your gift. The purpose of life is to give it away.' It is said that we make a living by what we get but we make a life by what we give. It is a well-established fact that, to be happy in life, we need to create happy vibes around us. To serve others has been considered one of the most important aspects of human life.

The Purpose of Life

I find it apt to quote Ralph Waldo Emerson's famous words once again. He said, 'The purpose of life is not to be happy. It is to be useful, to be honourable, to be compassionate, to have it make some difference that you have lived and lived well.'

Everybody tries their best to make their life and the life of their near and dear ones joyful and comfortable. We acquire a good education, pursue a rewarding career and buy a good house, nice car and so many other objects of utility and comfort to make ourselves happy.

Serving Others

It is a common experience that material acquisitions cease to give us any thrill after some time and soon after acquiring them life again seems dull and mundane. If we help someone in dire need of words of comfort, money, or any other kind of assistance, it gives us a lasting happiness. A life spent serving others is the best life. All societies and religions have extolled the act of serving others and held it to be the highest virtue of a human being.

An Exalted Act

Most of us are busy in our own survival and acquiring the means of comfort to make ourselves happy. Over a period, we reach a point of saturation where whatever we do or acquire does not add to our happiness, and life seems quite empty and joyless. It seems that something is missing and there is no zest or joy in life.

For real joy, we need to look beyond our own interests and be of some use or service to others. Once we start thinking of others, we find that life changes. We grow and become better persons. Serving others has always been an exalted act, as it not only helps people in need and distress but also sets a precedent to be emulated by others.

Being Happy Forever

Mahatma Gandhi said, 'The best way to find yourself is to lose yourself in the service of others.' The truth of this maxim was proved by the noble acts and the life of Mahatma Gandhi and many of his followers that ultimately resulted in our freedom from centuries-old colonial rule.

Those who dedicate their life to a worthy cause and spend it in serving others are found to be the happiest people. The best test of a society, its culture and civilization lies in the way it cares for its helpless and distressed persons. Success in wealth, material comforts and position in life gives happiness for some time, whereas helping others gives us a lifetime of happiness.

> **Learning Points:**
> - We make a living by what we get, but we make a life by what we give.
> - Material acquisitions give happiness for some time, and soon life again seems dull and mundane.
> - The best way to find yourself is to lose yourself in the service of others.

Acknowledgements

This book, *The Art of Joyful Living*, would not have been possible without the support and encouragement of close family and friends. I extend my sincere thanks and gratitude to them. The love and support of my wife and children have been a constant source of strength and creativity for me. These have enabled me to face the challenges of life with joy and equanimity, and have also inspired me to share my views and experiences with the readers.

I consider myself to be a serious student of life, and the questions of joy and happiness have always been of great curiosity and interest to me. I wish to appreciate the role of my wife Sharda, my dear children—sons Abhishek and Divya, and daughter Prashasti—their spouses and, above all, my grandchildren, who have made this journey, especially in this post-superannuation period of my life, full of joy and happiness.

I extend my gratitude to friends and colleagues, who have always been there to share the ups and downs of life, and have motivated me to record and share my thoughts and experiences about joy and happiness.

My thanks are also due to Rudra Narayan Sharma and Aditi Mehrotra of Rupa Publications for their valuable support and efforts in this creative journey. I would like to record my sincere gratitude to Kapish Gautam Mehra for the help and encouragement in this endeavour. My special thanks are due to the entire team at Rupa for their excellent efforts in bringing out the book in such an attractive and impressive form.

www.ingramcontent.com/pod-product-compliance
Lightning Source LLC
Chambersburg PA
CBHW020232170426
43201CB00007B/396